NEW EDITION

A Memoir

HITCHHIKING TO MADNESS

CAROL HAMILTON

Praise for *Hitchhiking to Madness*

"Carol's life was way harder than she had imagined it would be. She found many kind strangers, but her own resourcefulness was her greatest asset. This story gives us reason to notice young women and to listen to them. Carol has never stopped re-sculpting her own life. She has roamed with purpose and explored with delight. Her trajectory is something to sing about."

— Ellen Andrews, MD, Psychiatrist, Neurologist, Palliative Care

"Hamilton's inspirational memoir, *Hitchhiking to Madness*, is hard to put down. Fans of Kerouac's *On the Road* will be intrigued by four college drop-out Jesus freaks hitchhiking thousands of miles while searching for God's messages. When Hamilton finally escapes this hell, she rises to a position of academic success beyond what most doctors only aspire to. Her final gift is to organize the chaos of severe mental illness for those of us who haven't lived with and struggled to make sense of it."

— Mark Anthony Powers, MD, Pulmonology and Critical Care
Medicine, author of *A Swarm in May* and the Phineas Mann series

"*Hitchhiking to Madness* tells a compelling story with raw, honest, personal insight into the world of severe and persistent mental illness forced upon a naive twenty-something, just out to make the world a better place and find meaning through religion and spirituality. Readers go along for the ride of personal discovery, struggling, along with the author, to figure out what is happening to her good-hearted husband, and where the dividing line is between spirituality and psychosis. I recommend this book to all readers, especially to those involved with the world of mental health."

— Gordon Lipscomb, MSW, Clinical Social Worker, retired

"I first crossed paths with Dr. Carol Hamilton in 1996, when I was a medical student at Duke. She modeled compassion and humanity for my patient with AIDS. Now, reading *Hitchhiking to Madness*, I am astonished and humbled by Carol's compassion, wisdom, humanity, and clarity. As a practicing internist-psychiatrist I appreciate the time and effort she puts into describing her experience as her husband became more and more ill with schizophrenia, and as an observer of a disordered healthcare system I appreciate the light she sheds on the difficulties patients and their loved ones experience trying to obtain effective treatment. As a medical educator, I cannot speak highly enough of this book. I think it should be required reading for all seeking a career in clinical medicine."

— Jane P. Gagliardi, MD, MHS, Professor of Psychiatry and
Behavioral Sciences, Professor of Medicine

"What do you do when your intelligent and devoted husband, seemingly overnight, turns into a man you do not recognize? What if God doesn't have the answer? When do you put yourself before others? These are the questions at the heart of Hamilton's memoir, *Hitchhiking to Madness*, and the reason I could not put it down.

With wit, suspense, and excruciating candor, Hamilton weaves a tale that is at once exciting and horrifying. Like many young people in the '70s, Hamilton and her husband took to the road seeking the perfect spiritual home. But Hamilton's quest turned into a nightmare no one saw coming. Hamilton worked her way through heartbreak, disillusionment, and confusion to become the powerful woman she is today. This is a heartwarming and inspiring journey of a brave young woman. I highly recommend it."

— Danna Byrom, ESOL Faculty,
Austin Community College, Austin, Texas

"Dr. Carol Hamilton married her high school sweetheart at a young age. Her husband fell into the depths of schizophrenia during their journey of young marriage and parenthood. This well-written, fast-paced book is one family's journey to hell and back. It is the story of resilience, hard work, family support, and never giving up on yourself or your goals and dreams. It is a book you cannot put down!"

— Barbera Skipper, Ed.D., Superintendent of Leakey Independent
School District (retired), author of *Amasa Clark's Journey*
and *Doing Naturalistic Inquiry*

"Carol's book about her early adult life is heartbreaking yet astonishing. It is so well written you can almost feel the emotional roller coaster of love, sadness, and fear that she went through. It is educational as she describes many of the struggles of mental illness and post-traumatic stress."

— Cindy Rice, Compensation Analyst, retired

"This book pulled me in within the first couple of pages and kept my interest and attention throughout the author's journey (physically and mentally) during the early '70s. It is a testament to anyone finding themselves straying down the wrong path and making a determined decision to choose a different path."

— Markus Sorrells, Meterologist and Senior Configuration
Management Specialist supporting NOAA and NASA
with their weather satellites

To Jeffrey D. Green (1950–2013)

Years and years ago, and now I know.
The him who was him was so sad
to be lost in the tangles of his mind.

CONTENTS

CHAPTER 1

MURDEROUS INTENT, PART 1

December 1974, San Antonio, Texas

Sounds came from behind the door—the rustling of bed clothes, a cough, a thud—my husband rising from the mattress on the floor.

That's OK, I thought. *It's daylight now.*

I tensed under the blankets on the sofa, facing the bedroom door, waiting for him to emerge and reveal his state of mind.

"Oh, you're out here," Jeff said. He squinted in the light, trying to focus on where I was and remember why I might not be in bed with him. He had slept in his blue jeans, but his feet were bare. I saw memories and reactions click into place.

"It was a rough night," he said and looked away. He slid down the fake paneled wall and sat on the green shag carpet, his knees hugged to his chest.

I sat up on the sofa and leaned forward. I kept the pillow and blanket bunched around me. Lame protection, but it was all I had.

"Yeah, it was a rough night," I said. My voice was hoarse, and my eyes were probably puffy. But Jeff seemed approachable, grounded. I needed to make a move before I lost him.

"You know, Jeff, I was thinking that it feels like we're in a pressure cooker. We're all alone out here in this rented trailer house, in this weird mostly empty neighborhood, with all our family across town," I said. I gestured to the window where we could see a monotonous line of other fenced-in trailer houses for at least a mile in each direction. There were no trees but an occasional dog barking in someone's yard and a skinny guy walking briskly up the road with his jacket collar turned up, cigarette smoke trailing behind.

"It's Friday, and I can skip my one class today," I said. "Let's go stay with your folks for the weekend. We can eat your mom's pot roast, and maybe you can go hunting with your brother. I think we need to be around more people and relax a little; give ourselves a break."

He picked at his thumbnail. I pleated the sheet between my fingers, smoothed it out, and started again.

"Yeah, good idea. Let's get out of here," he said. He stood up and took his key ring out of his pocket, pacing while he twirled the keys around his finger.

"OK, great! Let me just grab a few things and I'm ready to go," I said and threw off the blankets. I stuffed a change of clothes and toiletries into the army surplus pack I had hitchhiked with and then grabbed my school backpack, untouched since coming home yesterday. I picked up my pillow from the sofa and turned, hoping he had unlocked the door, but saw he had stopped to read a passage from his Bible, absently fingering the keys.

Please, dear God, do not let him put the keys back in his pocket.

He looked up. "You ready?" he said. I nodded, and he unlocked the door. I was out but not yet safe.

"Jeff! Slow down! You're going to get us killed!" I said after he barely missed another other car's bumper.

"Don't be such a worry wort! Trust me, Susie. All you do is doubt and question everything. Have faith! Ever heard of that, Susie? Faith! You have to give it over, Susie, give it over to Jesus," he said.

"You're right, Jeff. You're right. I'm going to pray, and I'm sure the Lord will take care of us," I said.

I buried my face in my pillow.

Please, dear God, keep us safe. Keep this little baby inside my womb healthy and safe. Shield her till her daddy gets back to his normal, loving self. Please bring back the man I married, the man I love. Please help him stop making like I'm the enemy. And right now, please put a bubble around our car so we don't die in a crash. In Jesus's name, amen.

We finally arrived in front of my in-laws' house, a good thirty-min-ute drive from northwest San Antonio to the south side of town where Jeff and I had each grown up. It was still early on a Friday morning, but the family was in a typical frenzy to get Jeff's three younger brothers off to school.

"Well, look what the cat drug in!" my mother-in-law said when we walked through the front door. Malvis gave me a warm hug and tried to make eye contact with Jeff. Walter, Jeff's dad, looked out from the kitchen.

"What's up, son?" Malvis said. "You look frazzled! Want something to eat? I was just cleaning up the pan, but I can make more scrambled eggs. Sit down, y'all. Walter, put some more bread in the toaster, will ya'?"

"Boys! It's time for y'all to get going or you're going to be late for school!" Malvis hollered down the hall.

The normal bustle and banter washed over me, and I began to relax. We grabbed coffee and plates of food, and by the time we sat down, the kids were gone and the house sighed with relief.

"We've had a rough week," I said, once we'd eaten our fill. "We were hoping we could stay here for a few days and see if—"

"She wants to stay here," Jeff said, "'cause she's scared. But not me; I got things to do." I was surprised he said it, but I took the opening.

"Why do you think I'm scared, Jeff?" I asked.

"You're scared that you'll finally see the truth. You want Mom and Dad to help talk me into settling. 'Settle down and be a daddy,' 'Settle down and be my husband,' That's all you talk about. 'Get a job and get your mind off things,' you say. But I don't want to settle! Because that's not what the *Lord wants*! And I only want to have my mind on one thing, the Lord! Nobody else seems to remember that. Nobody else cares about that, but I do! I've got to spread His Word, and He won't let me rest until I do it."

"Son," his mother said, "what do you think Jesus wants you to do? You want to start going back to church? Our new congregation would accept you, I'm sure. Do you want to try to be a youth leader, like you were doing before? Or do you think—"

"No, church is not the answer, Mom," Jeff said. "The Church of Christ and other churches are filled with men who want power. They're the moneychangers in the temple. They've got nothing to do with God. You're just like everybody else, Mom. No one understands it, but it's getting clearer and clearer to me every day. And I know it's on me! Things are starting to happen, big things, and no one will be spared. Not you, not me, not some little baby in Susie's belly. I've got to warn people." Jeff was pacing now, pushing the dining room chairs in and pulling them out as he passed by each one, slamming some into the table.

"OK, Jeff, you can just calm down now," Walter said. "Why can't you stand up for Jesus and be a Christian at the same time you're working at a job, son? I agree with Susie. You need to stop all this talking and get to work! Besides which, what exactly do you want to do? Stand on the street corner? What are you going to say?"

Walter was a big man with a big voice and was prone to bluster. But at this moment, I was happy to have his support.

"See, that's the problem, Dad," Jeff said. "You're all the same. You've got to try to pin me down, argue me out of it, don't you? But I know what you're up to. I've been warned. I know your tricks. But just like Moses, I don't have to know the exact words beforehand. When the time's ready, the Lord will speak through me and say the right words. A few days ago, the Lord's voice was crystal clear in my head, and I know we've got to pray and spread the Word or it will get real ugly, real fast. But then when I get home with Susie, all I hear is her words to 'settle here and settle there,' and I've got to resist. I've got to say, 'Get thee behind me, Satan!' I've got to resist her womanly wiles."

He kept pacing and talking more to himself. "No one else can see what I see, and it's coming fast. It's coming fast. And then sometimes I can't hear His voice, and that's when the Devil gets a foot in the door. But he's smart, too, and I'm learning some things. Yeah, I'm learning a lot of things from him too . . .."

He went out the back door mid-sentence, and we could see him walking the perimeter of the backyard, talking to himself and now and then reaching down to pet the current family dog, a long-haired mutt who was jumping up and down in delight to see Jeff again.

I looked at Malvis and Walter and was glad they had witnessed one of his harangues.

"You can tell it's getting bad," I said. "I kept thinking he was going to snap out of it if only I prayed hard enough. But this is how he is now. How can God let his mind wander this way when all we ever wanted was to worship Him and serve Him and do the Lord's will? I keep thinking that if he were to just get a job and not have so much time on his hands—"

"I don't think this is about religion, Susie," Malvis said. "Like I've been saying these past few weeks, I think he's got a serious mental problem. He looks too much like the patients I see on the hospital ward at work, and it scares me." Malvis worked as an attendant at the State Mental Hospital and had been making the case to me that Jeff's behavior might be something serious, mental illness of some kind.

"I don't think he's just going through a bad patch," she said, "but when we talked the other day, you said he was doing better. You sounded happy, and I was hoping things were going back to normal."

"It's so up and down," I said. "For a while he would have four or five good days to every bad day. On good days he spends the morning out looking for work, and at supper time we talk about his prospects, my school stuff, and our plans with the baby. On bad days he hardly looks at me or touches me, and if I press him, he barks something about how I just don't understand or have enough faith and then gets in the car and drives off. When he comes back, it's like a rainstorm passed and the sun is out again. He will say something like he's prayed about it, everything is OK, and he's happy to be home."

We watched Jeff walking around in the backyard, occasionally bending down and digging in the garden. We couldn't tell if he was digging something up or burying something.

"Like I told Mom earlier this week, my mantra has become 'If Jeff is in a bad place, be patient. The storm will pass, and he'll get better. But if he's in a good place, be worried, because things are about to get bad.' But now, there are few good days and mostly bad ones," I said. "In fact, the cycles happen in the span of one day! He's crazy in the morning, good by afternoon, and a demon at night."

"And what really worries me," I said, "is that he now believes both God and Satan are talking to him, and they're convincing him that I'm the enemy, that I'm somehow doing Satan's bidding by trying to talk him into acting normal, or whatever you call it. Apparently, I'm evil because I want him to stay home with me, his wife, act like a husband, get a job, and get ready to be a dad!"

Malvis got up and poured herself another cup of coffee. I took a deep breath and continued.

"Last night was horrible," I said. "I'm not ready to tell you everything that happened, but it was bad, and I was scared. Until last night, no matter how crazy he was talking, I could eventually reach the real Jeff and get him to really see me. But not last night. I couldn't reach him. I didn't know who or what I was dealing with, but the Jeff I knew was gone. The man who was in his place was mean and hurtful and didn't care about me. I can't go back to that trailer house with him." I paused to wipe tears from my cheeks; my words were thick now, and it was hard to keep my voice from cracking.

"Also, I'm so worried he'll do something in public that will get him hurt or killed, because people won't understand what he's saying or trying to do. I completely agree with you now, Malvis—he is sick, and we have to get him help, whether he wants it or not," I said.

"OK, honey, I have the night shift at the hospital tonight, so let me try to talk to one of the doctors and figure out what we need to do. And let me do the dishes. You look beat. Go back and lay down on my bed and get some sleep," Malvis said. I took a shower first, changed into clean clothes, and then lied down. My brain was finally shutting down when I felt her put a blanket over me and close the door.

The next day Jeff was up early and left the house before we could stop him, but he seemed calm and we weren't too worried. I asked to borrow a car and went to the library where I worked all morning. I was a senior at Incarnate Word College, with a major in biology. The fatigue of early pregnancy and the chaos of Jeff's deteriorating mental state was taking its toll on my schoolwork.

When I got home, Malvis and I walked out back and looked over her garden, giving us privacy so she could tell me what she'd learned at work the night before. The doctors she worked with told her we had to get Jeff seen by a psychiatrist and then, even if Jeff refused his help, the psychiatrist who examined him could attest to his mental state and file for commitment papers. The commitment papers would lead to someone picking him up and taking him to the hospital. She had a plan for trying to get him to agree to see a doctor. We walked back into the house to find Jeff.

"And in other news today," the newscaster said from the TV blaring in the living room, "observers in Roswell, New Mexico, have reported sightings of flashing lights in the nighttime desert sky that coincided with electrical power surges in nearby neighborhoods. This is not the first unidentified flying object, or UFO, reported in the vicinity and probably not the last. US government officials could not be reached for comment, but scores of people in the vicinity confirmed the unusual nature of the sightings. And that's it for the nightly news—"

"*See!* I knew it!" Jeff said to his dad and brothers who were draped about on living room chairs, rug, and sofa. "Didn't I tell you today, Dad? Didn't I say they told me, 'Watch the sky. Just watch the sky'? That's what they meant! I just needed to watch and listen for a sign that they are coming from the sky! And there it was, given right in front of all of you, on the TV, so it's plain to see, for all who can see it. Oh, yes, God's got some mysterious partners, but who are we, you know? Who are we to question Him? *Wow!* That's it; that's it! And you are my witnesses!"

"Jeff, stop standing in front of the TV!" Walter said. "I can't hear what they're saying with you shoutin' and talkin' all over the place. Just sit down!"

Malvis walked over to Jeff, who was walking back and forth between the kitchen and living room, looking up to the heavens and whispering, "Thank you, Jesus! Thank you!"

"Son, can I talk to you in the kitchen for a minute?" Malvis said. She took Jeff by the elbow and guided him to the table. He was grinning like a Cheshire cat, but she looked serious.

"Jeff, I'd like you to go with me and Susie to see a psychiatrist this afternoon. I just found out that there's always one on-call over at the hospital emergency room, and I really think you need to talk to someone."

"But, Mom, didn't you hear the news?" Jeff said. "It proves just what I've been saying! I'm not crazy! I've got a special channel to the Lord, so I'm able to tell what's going on, and here's the proof! I need to use that channel now! I've got a responsibility to be God's messenger! It's not my choice, Mom. I really wish it wasn't me, but I've got no choice. Don't you see? I thought you'd be happy to know that I'm not just making it up! It's real, Mom! They sent me a message right there on national news!"

Malvis tightened her grip on his arm and touched his face, getting him to look her in the eyes.

"Jeff, I don't ask you for much, do I?" she said. He looked down at his feet. "Do I?"

"No, Mom."

"Honey, please do it for me, for your mother. Come with us to see the psychiatrist. What's it going to hurt? It will make me feel better if we get a professional opinion. Will you do it for me?" Malvis said.

Jeff agreed, to our surprise, and we went to the hospital, though he was cocksure that we were the crazy ones, not him.

"It's been two hours! I'm not waiting here another minute! This has been a complete waste of time!" Jeff said for the tenth time. He was pacing, and we were straining to catch the clerk's eye at the nurse's station, fearing they had forgotten us.

"Green? Jeff Green?" the clerk said, finally. We leapt out of our chairs and walked back to the exam room where we waited for another forty-five minutes. The door opened just as Jeff's patience was on the last thread.

"Mr. Green, a pleasure to meet you. And you are?" the doctor said. We introduced ourselves and prepared to launch into our litany of concerns, but he interrupted.

"Mr. Green, what brings you to see us today?"

The doctor was in his early thirties, thin, with a prominent Adam's apple, and he had a pronounced tic. Every twenty to thirty seconds his head would jerk toward the center, followed by an upward jerk of his right shoulder and a wink of his right eye. This was usually followed by a graceful movement of his left hand sweeping any ruffled hair away from his eyes. When he introduced himself, we could see that his right eye was permanently fixed looking inward, making eye contact with him . . . confusing. He turned and focused entirely on Jeff, who appeared to be stifling a laugh.

"Well, doc, my mom and my wife thought I needed to talk to a shrink because they think I'm crazy," Jeff said. If he thought his flippant remark would ruffle the doctor's feathers, he was mistaken.

"OK. Do you think you're crazy, Mr. Green?"

"No! I think I have important work to do, and so does the Lord! But every time I'm about to get down to business, somebody stands in my way and tries to get me off track."

"How do you know what God wants you to do, Mr. Green? Do you hear voices telling you to do certain things?" the doctor said.

"Of course not! I pray, just like every other Christian. It's just that I've got good at listening," Jeff said.

"Do you see things that other people can't see, like visions from God? Sometimes we call these visual hallucinations?" the doctor asked.

"No, sir! I just see these people trying to make me live the way they want me to live instead of how I know I'm supposed to be living, telling others about the word of God," Jeff said.

"Have you ever considered harming yourself?" the doctor asked.

"You mean like suicide? No, sir, that would be against the commandments which say to keep our bodies healthy and pure because they are a temple to God," Jeff said.

"Have you considered hurting your wife, or another person, maybe because they were getting in your way of doing the important work God wants you to do?" the doctor asked.

"No," Jeff said. "No, sir." He was on a roll. And he was crazy, crazy like a fox.

"Well, then," the doctor said, "I don't see that I have that much to offer—"

"Wait a minute! We have some things to add, doctor!" I said. "Just today he was convinced that God sent him a message through the TV about UFOs in New Mexico! And he is obsessed with this idea of 'doing the Lord's work', so much so that he won't go look for a job because he's convinced that's not what he is supposed to be doing. But he's not applying to be a preacher somewhere or planning to go to preacher school; he just says he needs to 'spread the word'! And lately he's saying that it's not just God who's telling him stuff, it's the devil too, and the devil is telling him that I work with him—the devil!—because I am wanting Jeff to act like normal, like he used to, and be a loving husband and father to-be. His talk is not normal, doctor! It's crazy talk!"

Malvis broke in and added more examples of his abnormal behavior and speech, but Jeff interrupted both of us.

"See, doctor, they just don't agree with me, and that's a problem. But also, I have to admit; I've been pretty down lately and get kinda irritated and haven't been the nicest to my wife, Susie. I think it's because I haven't found a job yet, and I've had too much time on my hands. I know they're just worried for me, and I'm going to get a job this next week. For sure, I'm going to get a job. Y'all can just stop worrying about it. I'm alright now. I can see I've got you both real worried. Let's just go home and make a fresh start. How about it?" Jeff said. Malvis and I looked at each other. Wow, what a great ploy.

"I'm sorry, Mrs. Green, that you and your husband are having these marital problems," the doctor said, looking at me. "I can recommend a marriage counselor, but I don't see anything that I need to deal with here in the emergency room. Jeff denies hearing voices or having visual hallucinations, says he is not planning to harm himself or others, and seems to have a good idea of what's going on. But if anything changes, and if you want to come in and talk to me later next week, Jeff, I'm happy to see you again. Here's my card, and it's been good to meet you all."

Malvis and I trailed a little behind Jeff as we walked down the green and white hospital corridor out toward the car, shaking our heads.

"Well, that was a waste of time!" Malvis said.

"The whole thing was absurd," I said.

Jeff turned around and grinned.

"Like I said, who's the crazy one?" Jeff said and perfectly mimicked the doctor's tic and crossed eyes.

We couldn't help ourselves; Malvis and I burst out laughing and the three of us relished a moment of hilarity and release of tension at the poor doctor's expense.

The next morning was Sunday, and Malvis and Walter went to church. She and I had decided there was nothing we could do on a Sunday and planned to start calling psychiatrist offices the next day, trying to find someone who specialized in acute mental illness who could advise us what to do next. The boys got a reprieve from having to get up early and go to church since I was still not keen on being alone with Jeff or letting him too far out of my sight. Malvis's pot roast simmered in the oven, and I worked on schoolwork while they were gone. Jeff was intensely busy, though doing what, I wasn't sure. At one point he was looking in every drawer in the house and the garage and the bins in the storage sheds, eventually coming out with what looked like a block of steel in his hands.

"What are you looking for, Jeff?" I asked.

"Oh, nothing much. Just seeing what's here. You can always find what you need if you look hard enough," he said. "The Lord always provides!"

He had a little sing-song falsetto note in his voice. I shivered. What did his voice remind me of?

"What are you doing, Susie? Being a good teacher's pet?" Jeff said, a little while later.

"Teacher's pet? Hardly," I said. "I'm so far behind! I've got to turn in an outline on my senior research project tomorrow. I have fifty more pages to read in parasitology by Tuesday and a unit test in comparative anatomy at the end of the week." I sounded like a prig even to my own ears. So be it; I was a serious student and hated not being prepared.

"Susie, always such a busy little bee," he said. I heard him whistling as he went to the spare bedroom off the dining room. I shivered again. Maybe I'm catching a cold?

I enjoyed the mid-afternoon Sunday dinner and the bustle of having family close by, but Jeff became more brooding and confrontational as it ended. He and his dad exchanged harsh words, and everyone was glad to go to their separate rooms for the evening to read or talk to friends on the telephone.

A while later, Jeff called to me from the spare bedroom where he'd been busy all day.

"Hey, Susie! Come back here. I have something to show you," he said.

I put the highlighter in the book I was reading, got up, and stretched before walking back to where he was. It was an odd request, but I needed a break. I was falling asleep reading about identification properties of tapeworm eggs.

He stood in the doorway and ushered me into the bedroom with a flourish. I didn't see anything obvious that he might have been working on, but before I could ask, I heard the keys turn in the door handle. I heard the click of a lock.

I whirled around, my heart pounding. "Why did you lock us inside the bedroom, Jeff?"

I watched him put the keys deep in his front jeans pocket. Again?

"Just a little surprise, Susie," he said. The sing-song voice . . . déjà vu from the night at the trailer house.

"Just sit here next to me, Susie," he said. He took my hand and pulled me over to the twin bed where he made me sit next to him. "We've got some business to take care of you know?" His voice had lost its sing-song quality, and his eyes had turned flat. Dr. Jekyll was gone; Mr. Hyde was in charge.

"What business are you talking about, Jeff?" I said. My entire body started to shake.

"Game's up, Susie," he said. "Miss Perfect, Miss Sunshine, Miss Mommy-to-be! I need to see the baby now, because I know what you've been doing behind my back. I *know* the baby's not mine." I was speechless and then incredulous. But before I could protest, he went on.

"You know," he said, "I kept trying to figure out why God would put a baby in my path when He wants me to be doing His will, not the will of mankind, or what my earthly wife wants me to do. And then it came to me in prayer, of course! It's not my baby! It can't be my baby; the Lord wouldn't let it be! And when I bring the baby out of your belly, everyone will know the Jezebel you really are because he'll have the mark of Satan on him. He'll be as black as black can be, the Devil's son!" His eyes were fixed on me, and I could see that he believed what he was saying, with his whole heart. And it had a sick logic to it—if your wife had the Devil's baby in her belly, you would be a saint if you destroyed it. He wanted to be that saint.

"Jeff, what are you talking about? Of course, it's your baby! I've never been with another man in my life! But it's too early to see the baby, hon; it won't be born until next May. But you can feel your baby! Here, put your hand here," I said, trying to make his crazy talk into something under-standable, normal, sane. I tried to take his hand from my wrist, but he kept a tight grip and would not let me place it on my belly.

Then, he leaned forward, pressing against me, just for a moment. He pulled back, and the pillow dragged along the bed behind me until it stopped against my back and on top of my hand, soft and cool. Jeff sat back with a sad but satisfied smile on his face, the knife in his hand.

If I were a cinematographer, Jeff would get blurry at this point and the camera would zoom in on my face, follow the movement of my eyes. Jeff's words would slow down and come from far away, something about Satan and "out of the womb." The sound of my heart would obliterate all else. The camera would pan down the length of the eighteen-inch Bowie knife I had given Jeff a few years ago as a birthday present; it would stop at the glint of oil still visible along the knife's edge. The viewer would see my nostrils flare as I smelled machine oil—and the penny dropped. Rifling in the drawers, the steel block in his hand—a whetstone—the knife was honed and ready to go. Premeditated.

How had we gotten here, on the precipice of tragedy? We were just kids who, until a few months ago, were hitchhiking across America, seeking spiritual truth and a life of worship and service. We learned much but found no Godly community to live with, no "One Truth," as it were. Jeff had gone from bright and curious to dark and unstable, spinning out of control. Now, within a span of five days, my husband had held me captive, raped me, and was threatening to mutilate if not murder me to prove our baby was the spawn of Satan.

We had not found a path to God and a Heavenly reward.

We had hitchhiked straight to hell.

CHAPTER 2

THE ROAD TO HELL

1950s to 1970s, San Antonio, Texas

Our road to hell was paved with the best intentions. Two years before I found myself at the dangerous end of a Bowie knife, Jeff and I were a young married couple living a conventional life. I was a full-time college student, and he was a lineman for the telephone company in San Antonio. I was a Sunday school teacher, and he was an assistant leader of the church youth group at a local Church of Christ. But when we began seeking a kinder, less judgmental version of Christianity, our search threatened the church's leadership and their authority. The preacher pushed to excommunicate us, leading to our departure from traditional religion and an orthodox life.

The preacher of the Highland Hills Church of Christ stood about 5'4" tall and had a diminutive wife and a daughter my age. He looked perpetually tan—golf course plus genetics, I assumed—and had malleable-looking skin like a hound dog's that easily stretched into an engaging smile or a furrowed look of disapproval. He had been the preacher since I first started coming to church in elementary school.

His motives for getting us kicked out of his church were as old as human society: we threatened his authority and reputation and, thus, his livelihood. An animal whose territory is at risk may claw, bite, or sting. Humans may duel, divorce, or murder, whatever it takes to neutralize the threat. It should not have come as any great surprise to us, then, but it did. And when we were excommunicated, or "disfellowshipped," which is the term the Church of Christ uses, it pulled loose the first thread of Jeff's unraveling. The event shocked and grieved me, for sure, but it was more than that for him.

I did not grow up going to church. My parents considered themselves Christians but did not fret much about the details. My dad, Fred, worked full time, plus one or two extra jobs as a freelance machinist, making time off on Sundays especially precious. Edith, my mom, and her eight siblings grew up under their mother's Baptist restrictions against drinking, dancing, and card playing, which they uniformly rejected as adults. Dad's occasional brush-up with church people as a child involved what he called "holy rollers" in California, and they frightened him and his brother. Mom and Dad were also distrustful of the holier-than-thou judgmental attitude of the churchgoers they knew. We did celebrate major Christian church holidays, though, which for me were the perfect mix of new clothes my mother sewed, yummy food, candies, and mystery. We sometimes went to church with Grandma on those occasions, and we always ended up at her house to join aunts, uncles, and cousins where adults and kids played baseball or football and cousins shared booty from Santa Claus or the Easter bunny.

Photo 1: Cousins Martha (my right) and Barbara (my left), Easter, circa 1955.

Our spotty church attendance meant that I was not burdened by much specific Christian dogma or the concepts of sin and guilt, and I had no hesitation about making up my own religious rites and rules. I figured that, if Jesus loved me, like the song said, He would love me even if I got some details wrong. I remember evenings pressing my nose into the bedroom window screen, watching the full moon rise over our neighbor's house. I was convinced Jesus lived in that moon, and I prayed to Him on those occasions.

"Dear Jesus," I said, "school was awful today. I thought Beverly was my very best friend, but then Nancy told me Beverly had a birthday party on Saturday, and I wasn't invited. It's not fair! What did I do wrong? She likes Larry, and I do, too. I can't help it that he gave me a note last week and asked me to be his girlfriend. What should I do? Please help me. Amen."

My religion was simple and sweet, and my imagined God gave love and protection, acceptance, and joy. In my religion, I didn't sweat the details. But in Texas at that time, many still thought it was proper for every child to be subjected to regular attendance at a Christian church, and what better place to pressure families than through their kids, at school?

"Class, class, look up here at me! Good morning!" Mrs. Ahr said and clapped her hands to get our attention.

Our third-grade teacher wore her hair long, even though she seemed too old for such a young hairdo. I wondered if she liked it long to try to hide her hairy forearms. Also, she had "pets" and I was one of them, which I soon learned was not a good thing. One day she would be weirdly chummy, taking me to the teachers' break room while she got coffee, making snippy remarks about other teachers or other students, like I was her best friend. I liked it very much the first time it happened, but the next day she was cold as ice toward me and chastened me when I acted familiar with her. It made me doubt myself. Had I just had imagined the other version of her? An early lesson in gaslighting.

"It's Monday morning! Are you all rested and ready for school today?"

"Yes, Mrs. Ahr," the class answered back in recitation.

"Good! Now, who went to church yesterday? Raise your hand if you went to church; everybody else, put your head on your desk. Now let me count . . ." This was the first, but would not be the last, time she put us through this exercise.

"James, tell me why you didn't go to church yesterday," she said.

He sat up to speak, but she interrupted him. "No, James, I did not say to lift your head off your arms. Just tell the class your answer with your head bowed on your arms. Go ahead now . . ."

James put his head back down on his arms and spoke, his voice muffled, his ears red.

"I don't know. My parents didn't have time, I guess?" he said.

"Mm, hmm," she said. Dismissing him, she looked for another target.

I prayed to baby Jesus in the manger and all the cuddly lambs as well. "Don't let her say my name. Please, don't let her say—"

"Carol Sue!" she said, calling me by my school name, not my family nickname, Susie. "You have your head down. I am disappointed in you. Why didn't you go to church on Sunday?" she asked, and in that moment, I knew that I would never forget the definition of two recent vocabulary words: shame and humiliation. I spoke with my head down, as instructed, addressing my desk, like James, and the embarrassment deepened.

"My dad has to work every day, including Saturday. Sunday is his only day to sleep late, and my mom says—" I began, but she interrupted me too. She had made her point.

"Well, there's lots of excuses around here today," she said. "You all better talk to your parents and let them know that going to church on Sunday is more important than sleeping late or watching football," she said. "Now open your social studies book to page 59, and Carol Sue, you can read us the next three pages since you had all that time to sleep in and rest yesterday while we were at church." I read the pages with an enormous lump in my throat and had to blink back tears so I could see the words.

Remembering the scene makes me angry today and an even more ardent supporter of our constitutional mandate for separation of church and state. Nevertheless, it had the desired result at the time. I wanted no more of the shame I felt that day. I wanted to belong to a church to show I was not one of *those* people. My opportunity came as a result of my parents spending time with our neighbors up the street, June and Art, who were teaching them to play bridge. Art and June were members of the local Highland Hills Church of Christ and invited us to come to church with them. My parents demurred, but I started going with them.

My affiliation with the Church of Christ was based on opportunity and coincidence, not on any informed decision making. My best neighborhood friend, Laurie, was Baptist, like my grandmother, and I'm not sure why I didn't become Baptist except that she had been going there since infancy and had an exclusive lock on potential friends I might have made there. I also had friends who went to the nearby Catholic school and to mass on weekends, but no one in our family was Catholic and I didn't much like the idea of having to eat fish on Fridays, which was still a requirement then and the reason our school cafeteria served smelly fish cakes on Fridays. The Church of Christ believed in things similar to my grandma's Baptist church—thus, familiar—and the people were welcoming. I formed friendships with the pre-teens and teens there, and the adults doted on me. I was eventually baptized, and the Highland Hills Church of Christ became my church.

"Hi, Mrs. Green," I said to my Sunday school teacher one evening at a church ice cream supper that Art and June took me to. It was almost summer, and the air was warm and starting to fill with fireflies drifting up from the grass near the fields. I was hoping she'd introduce me to the guy standing next to her whom I'd seen at church but had never met. He was cute!

"Well, hi there, Susie! It's so good to see you here! Who'd you come with? Oh, hey there, Art, June!" she said and waved to them before they made their way to the cakes, pies, and iced buckets full of hand-churned ice cream.

"Have you met my son?" Malvis Green asked. "This is Jeff, and that was his sister, Lori, who just walked that way taking ice cream to her boyfriend."

"Hi, I've seen you around," Jeff said. He had a great smile and looked good in a white short-sleeved oxford shirt, blue jeans, and loafers. "Grab some ice cream and let's go sit over there with the other kids so we don't have to be with the 'old folks,'" he said and tried to tickle his mom before she laughed and ducked away. I noticed his warm brown eyes and how he looked right into my eyes when we talked. Conversation was easy with him, and after our friends drifted away, we walked around a nearby baseball field, briefly touching hands. We were close enough that I noticed a whiff of cologne—English Leather?

"What's your favorite thing to do?" I asked.

"Play football," he said. "Go out to the woods with my .22 rifle. Go on dates with girls like you," he teased, and I rolled my eyes, blushed, and hoped it was true. "I'm just kidding. How old are you anyway?" he asked.

"I'm finishing seventh grade," I said. "How about you?"

"I'm finishing ninth grade and headed to high school in September. What do you do when you're not at school? I bet you're one of those brainy girls, right?"

"I like school if that's what you mean," I said. "And I've taken piano lessons since second grade, which I like, though I hate having to practice every day. And I'm in the school band where I play flute, but I just started that this year. Mostly I like hanging out with my friends, suntanning, and we just started going to Teen Town on weekends to listen to music and dance. But don't tell anyone here because they'll think I'm bad for dancing! Do you like to dance?"

"Nah, I don't dance. I never learned. It's a sin, ya know!" he said, but he was laughing and made it clear it wasn't a top-ten kind of sin in his book, mostly just unnecessary and boring.

Other than occasional brush-ups at church when I went with Art and June, I did not interact with Jeff after that occasion in 1965 until I was a sophomore, and he was a senior at the same high school. Jeff's home was just a few blocks from where I lived, but our childhoods were different in several important ways. I was an only child, while Jeff was one of five, the oldest son. When not working, my family's weekday routine included piano practice and homework for me, followed by the three of us sitting down to Mom's home-cooked supper together, having lively conversation. Every free minute before and after supper, I spent playing with neighborhood or school friends. Weekends were usually filled with family or friend dinners, bridge or pinochle playing for my parents, yard croquet or badminton, or fishing and camping trips at the coast.

Our lives were also different in terms of our parents' expectations. Neither of our parents had graduated from college, but mine expected me to do so, while Jeff's parents planned for their kids to go straight to work after high school graduation. I don't know how they did it, but my parents instilled in me a rock-solid belief that I could accomplish anything I set my mind to. Small successes, like learning to read before school, bred more success and confidence, I'm sure. In fact, books were a huge part of my young childhood, sparking my imagination and providing metaphors I could understand and build on. One of my most favorite books was *The Little Engine that Could.* I identified with the little train with his big heart, going beyond what anyone thought possible, carried up the hill by the desire to help others and by the force of his own self-determination. I remember playing on the backyard swing set going higher and higher saying, "I think I can! I think I can!" Reach the stars? Flip over the swing set? I'm not sure, but it was a mantra that I held on to my entire life.

I don't think Jeff felt special in the way I did, probably not surprising being one of five instead of the only child like I was. Jeff's family's social life revolved around church activities, their kids, and home life. His dad, Walter, was a deacon and Malvis a Sunday school teacher at the Highland Hills Church of Christ congregation, and they attended services Sunday mornings as well as most Sunday and Wednesday evenings. They read and studied the Bible and believed every word of it. They adhered to the church's doctrines to not drink alcohol or dance, but they weren't opposed to laughing and fun. And it was no secret that they had an active sex life, as evidenced by five kids, and condom wrappers in their parents' trashcan that the kids cringed over. Imagine, your parents having sex! Gross!

Jeff also read and believed in the Bible as an instruction manual for getting to heaven. Like his parents, he was not a preachy, self-righteous teen, but he could spout out the church's explanations for why their specific teachings were the only right way while other Christian denominations were likely sending their members to hell. He did not balk as much as his older sister did at being corralled into the family car for church so often.

"Hey, Mom, I want to read this chapter of the Bible when it's my turn in Sunday school," I imagine Jeff saying from the back seat of the station wagon over the ruckus of his siblings on their way to church one day. "This is from the Bible, for real: 'The curves of your thighs are like jewels . . . your navel is like a rounded bowl . . . and your breasts are like two fawns, twins of a gazelle.'"

"Whoa, no way!" say his brothers, Kim and Kyle, immediately interested in the conversation. His sister Lori rolls her eyes and goes back to reading her *Seventeen* magazine with no comment.

"Alright, alright, Jeff, that's enough. What are you reading? Psalms?" Walter says from the front seat before he checks his side mirrors and turns into the church parking lot.

"It's probably Song of Solomon, right, Jeff?" says Malvis.

"Yeah, Song of Solomon! Is that OK, Mom?" Jeff says and looks amused as he waits for her to squirm at the awkward predicament—her son reading a sex scene from the Bible out loud to his Sunday school class.

"Sure, son, go ahead. It's in the Bible, and there's nothing wrong with sex between a husband and a wife. There's a reason people have sex. It feels good, and God made it that way; so that means it's not evil *if* you're married! So, if you're comfortable reading that passage in front of your class, be my guest!" Malvis says.

Dang it. Trumped again. Why are moms so smart?

Malvis loved being part of the church community and had good church friends, but she knew there was plenty of room for improvement, including, and maybe especially, among the most faithful attendees. She did not truck with hypocrisy, and she tried to stay above the rumor mill, the unsanctioned but most common sport in social circles, including churches. I imagine a typical scene with Malvis at church.

"Well, she looks like she had a rough night," says Sherolyn, a young mother standing with Malvis and a few other women in the church foyer.

She gives a nod and sideways glance to a teen across the way. "I hear she's going out with a senior from Robert E Lee high school on the north side of town and that they stay out till all the movies are over at the drive-in, if you know what I mean." She bounces her fussy teething infant on her hip and looks like she could use a nap herself.

A little smile starts on Malvis's face, and one eyebrow quirks upwards.

"Sherolyn, dear, I believe I remember us standing here sayin' the very same thing about you when you and Eddie were dating not that long ago! But look how sweet you and your baby have turned out!" Sherolyn blushes and has the grace to admit that Malvis has a fair point but makes a mental note to take her gossip away from Malvis Green's earshot in the future. I imagine Malvis was not invited to the juiciest gabfests, but as far as I could tell, people loved and respected her for it.

So, while we both loved our church, in retrospect, I can see why being disfellowshipped might have affected us differently. The Church of Christ was my chosen religious affiliation, whereas it was part of Jeff's foundation. It was inextricably linked to his perceived place in the world. It was what made him feel chosen and right with God. I felt little hesitation to question church canon or inconsistencies in the Bible, and eventually that's what got us in trouble.

When I finally ran into Jeff again midway through my first semester of tenth grade, he remembered me. I had been keeping my eye out for him, and when we connected, I was certain I wanted to be his girlfriend. He was 5'10" in stocking feet but usually wore cowboy boots that made him closer to 5'11" to my 5'5"—a perfect fit. He had sandy brown hair that bleached blond in the summer, smooth, soft olive-complected skin, and full lips. I was starting to understand how important the sense of smell was to me, and I loved how he smelled. I loved his just-showered smell, his sweaty post-football smell, and his fresh outdoor smell. He was masculine in all the ways I liked: he loved to play sand lot football, preferred woodsy outdoor activities to anything indoors, and liked working on his car. He was wiry and muscular and had wonderful hands. Once we started going steady, he was not afraid to show me his softer side and taught me how to look at the natural world with wonder and curiosity. He also liked poetry and Shakespeare that he was exposed to in his senior English Lit class and gave me a poem he had copied from Robert Browning called "Summum Bonum." He had often observed bees flying flower to flower, flocked like a Christmas tree with pollen, and explained how evocative the first line of the poem was: "All the breath and bloom of the year in the bag of one bee . . ."

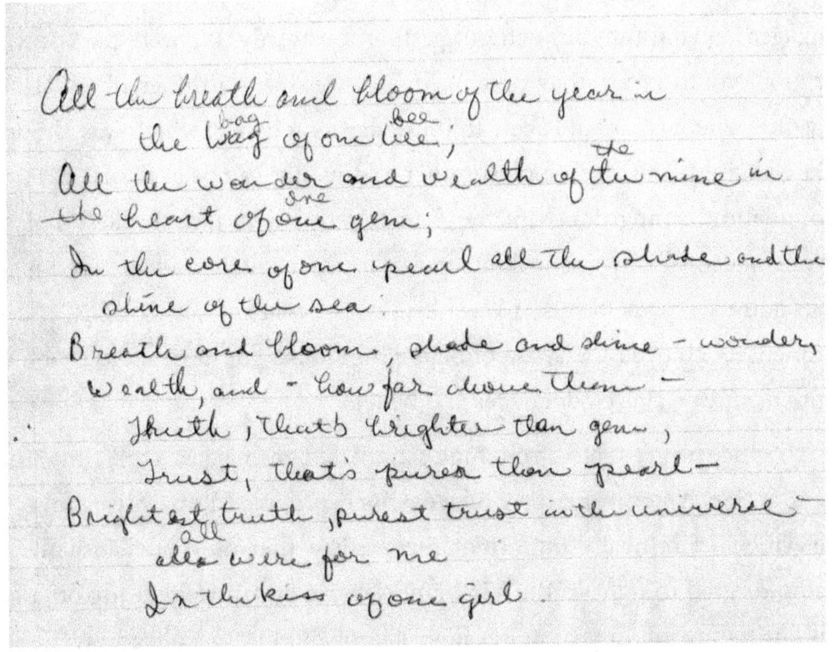

Photo 2: Jeff's handwritten copy of Robert Browning's poem "Summum Bonum" which he gave me when we started dating, circa 1968, his senior year of high school.

Soon we were meeting at lunch and sneaking out of the study hall to continue our conversations along a sunny no-man's-land corridor at school. A sophomore girl dating a senior boy carried a certain cache, so my social standing rose when I started seeing him, even though Jeff was not a particularly popular guy. I was not yet allowed to officially go on dates, but meeting up at church didn't count so we both became a lot more interested in being there. He had a car, and that became our private haven for intense conversations interspersed with steamy make-out sessions. Chaste kisses and hugs gave way to more compelling physical intimacy over time. We tried to abide by what we believed were Biblical standards for Christian behavior before marriage, but we mostly worked on "Night Moves" like Bob Seger sang about.

About this time, our congregation designated Bill, and his lovely wife Jane, as our youth group leaders. They were a young couple with no kids yet. They were solid, dependable, and instinctively knew how to keep teens engaged, having fun, but without getting too rowdy. We were part of the original youth group they organized, and we did fun things like skating parties (where you could skate to music holding hands, which was almost like dancing), and week-long summer and winter camps at the H. E. Butt Foundation campgrounds in the Frio River canyon near Leakey, Texas. We sang acapella hymns, volunteered at local hospitals, and attended picnics and ice cream socials. It was like having scores of new cousins, and I immensely enjoyed the sense of belonging. I also got more serious about understanding church doctrines and beliefs.

Once he graduated from high school, Jeff enrolled as a full-time student at San Antonio Junior College, which provided him with a college deferment, a critically important mechanism that prevented him from being drafted to fight in the Vietnam War. He and I went steady off and on during my junior year, me at high school and him in college, but I also enjoyed other high school-based flirtations and short-term romances. I was still very attracted to Jeff and trusted him with our increasingly intimate physical relationship, but by late in my junior year I was getting bored. He was silly when I wanted serious; he was laid-back when I was looking for more ambition and drive. And he never learned to dance!

I broke up with Jeff at the end of my junior year of high school so I could date other guys. I still thought maybe he was "the one," especially given our church connection, but I didn't want to narrow my choices so early in life. He was crushed, and I missed him, but I had an amazing summer when my parents and I went on a road trip to New Mexico and Colorado. The boys seemed to come out of the woodwork at the campgrounds, ice cream parlors, and national parks, drawn to the sixteen-year-old pheromones that I must have been emitting. I remember being flirted with by a ruggedly handsome cowboy on his way to the next rodeo near Ruidoso, a cerebral conversation with a blond-haired college guy on a road trip from school, and an offer to see a spectacular sunset, which I desperately wanted to accept.

I was walking along the road of one of the national parks we were camping in, and the sun was setting behind me. The convertible's tires squealed as the car came to a stop in the opposite lane.

"Hey, hi! How are you?" he said. "My name's Benjamin; Ben, they call me. What's yours?"

The sun was low in the sky, and his face was illuminated by its glow. Blond hair, straight white teeth, a dazzling smile . . . *What's that new actor's name? I was thinking. Robert Redmund or something?*

"My name is Carol. Nice to meet you, Ben," I said. I was smiling; he was smiling.

"Listen, I know this sounds like a pick-up line, but I saw the most spectacular sunset here last night, and I'm headed back to that spot right now. Want to jump in and see it with me?" he said.

"I'd love to! But I need to ask my folks. We're camped just around the bend, up there," I said.

"Oh, of course! I think I just passed them. I'll turn around and meet you there," he said and proceeded to do just that. I walked into our camp just as he parked and climbed out of the sports car.

"Hi, sir, ma'am, I'm Ben. I just met your daughter, Carol. I was wondering if you would give permission for me to take her for a drive up over the hill there to watch the sunset. I saw it last night, and it was spectacular," he said. Dad's smile faded as he released Ben from his handshake.

"No, sir, Ben, not today. You're probably a nice guy and all, but I don't know you, and I'm not at all comfortable with my daughter getting in a stranger's car and driving away," Dad said. I tried not to have a full-on temper tantrum while the best-looking guy I had ever seen was leaning against his red MGM convertible, being told no by my ridiculously over-protective dad.

"You're welcome to follow us there if that would make it alright," Ben said, going way farther than I would have imagined trying to get my dad to say yes.

I was grinning from ear to ear, but my dad was having none of it. I was infuriated, him treating me like a child! But I got over it when the guy returned to our campsite after he watched the sunset, alone, and we enjoyed a campfire and s'mores and fun conversation late into the evening.

"See, he was *not* an axe murderer!" I said later that night. But still, I knew Dad was just being a good dad.

On returning home later in the summer, I met a college guy whose dad was an officer at Brooks Air Force Base, ten minutes from our house. He had a buckskin horse stabled there, which he taught me to ride bareback. He was a serious but interesting and engaging young man, a couple years older than I, very respectful, and good looking. I was more and more certain that life without Jeff had excellent potential.

My senior year of high school was in full swing, with football games and dance parties and slumber parties most weekends. I liked my teachers and more challenging school subjects, and my girlfriends and I were starting to talk about colleges and majors and the like. I had my driver's license and my grandparents' old Pontiac to drive. The car was as big as a boat with huge tail fins and a finicky carburetor. It also carried the stench of spoiled milk the entire time I drove it. The smell that emanated from the trunk had been there since my grandfather's stroke caused him to crash the car while he was driving Grandma home from the grocery store. There was minor damage to the car and just a few bruises to my grandparents, but in the urgency to get Grandpa's stroke taken care of, the groceries in the trunk of the car were forgotten for several hot summer days. The event ended Grandpa's driving career, so I got to use the car. I had to hold my nose for the first five minutes of each drive, and my girlfriends teased me mercilessly every time we took my car to go someplace, but it was great to have the independence of wheels. We were back and forth to each other's houses all the time. We had heated debates about the major world events unfolding around us: the women's movement and what it meant for us, the Civil Rights Movement and recognition of the injustices done to native Americans, the Vietnam war. But we were optimistic that our generation could fix all the problems as soon as we were in charge.

It was a week or so after my seventeenth birthday when my idyllic, near-perfect childhood and adolescence came to an end. I was in the spare bedroom that doubled as my mom's sewing room and the new "Hi-Fi" music room, lying on the sofa, in the dark, listening to The Moody Blues sing "Nights in White Satin." It was after dinner, and my father knocked gently and asked to come in. He turned on the overhead light.

"*Daaad!* What? Can you turn off that light, please? Geez . . ." I said and squinted up at him in massive annoyance. He turned on the lamp in the corner by Mom's sewing machine and flipped off the overhead light. He knelt by the sofa and put his hand on my hair and face.

"I have something to talk to you about," he said. I turned to my side and faced him.

"Susie," he said, "I need to tell you something you probably are not going to like. But you must know I love you so much, and this is not about you. It's about me. I'm going to leave home for a while, just to take some time and try to figure some things out," he said.

I sat up, wary, but so unprepared for such words that I wasn't even alarmed yet. "You mean over the weekend or something? Like, you're going fishing by yourself or something? What are you talking about?" I said, even more annoyed that he was interrupting my reverie with something that sounded scary. He was the adult, and I was the kid. His job was to *not* scare me, ever.

I laughed a little, nervous, and said the most shocking and horrible thing I could think of, just to give the moment some levity.

"Geez, Dad, you sound like you're getting a divorce or something!"

"Well, I don't know. Maybe, but let's just see," he said.

Now I was alarmed. My heart lurched in my chest, and tears sprang to my eyes. I leaned forward and looked at him, really looked at him. He had to be kidding. It was an early Halloween trick or something, or I was having a nightmare. I needed to wake up. This happened to other people, not to us. I had never even seen my parents argue or yell at each other.

"Dad, what are you saying? Stop, please!" I said.

"I've lived half my life already," he said, "and almost that whole time, I've been married. Married and working and then having a child. Is that all there is to life? I feel like I've missed out on some important things. I need to figure out if this is all there is to life or if there's more. It feels like it's now or never. But I love you, and I will always be here for you and be your father. This has *nothing* to do with you."

CHAPTER 3

A NEST OF MY OWN

1969 to 1972, San Antonio, Texas

In the scope of the world's tragedies, my father's midlife crisis and our family's rupture were small problems. We were not beset by war or famine, neither parent was drug or alcohol addicted, and no one was abusive. I had a roof over my head and food on the table. But it rocked my world; it cracked my foundation. I felt shocked, blindsided, and sucker punched. My mother staggered under a mountain of grief and disbelief. She cried and screamed and did not try to hide her anger and sense of betrayal.

I racked my brain looking for clues I had missed indicating that he had been unhappy. My parents had always been nice to each other, though I realized it had been a while since I had seen them kissing or showing much affection to one another in our day-to-day lives. And now that I thought about it, Dad had been getting more and more snippy with Mom. Before he moved out, I confronted him.

"Dad," I said, "lately I've noticed that, when I roll my eyes and get sarcastic with Mom, you join in, like you're on my side. At first, I liked it, you and me laughing and joking together against the boring mother. But it's weird when you do it. It's like you're trying to act like a teenager, too. It makes me embarrassed to see you do it, and it hurts her feelings. And that's a mean thing for a husband to do, isn't it? Is that related to why you're moving out?"

"Yes," he said, "in a way, that's a good example. I guess I do kind of feel like a rebellious teenager, and she's my mom, making me be nice, follow the rules, and stay in line. And I agree it's not a nice way to act to your mama who is the most wonderful woman in the world and the best wife a man could possibly want. It's just me. I'm not happy, and I need to figure out why. You're right. It's not fair to her when I act like that."

Mom kept going over the details of their marriage, imagining where she went wrong and what she could have done differently.

"It started slowly, his discontent," she said, "but really got noticeable when we started playing bridge all the time with Kitty and Bill. Your dad started getting cool toward me then, and it was even more obvious when I saw how alive and flirty he got when Kitty was around."

"And I can't deny it; she's beautiful," Mom went on. "She knows how to make herself up and wears high heels and silk stocking and short skirts and can't help but show off her enormous breasts. But she's so young! How could he think she would even be interested in him? And my sorority sister! I tried saying something to Fred, but he told me I was imagining things and I just needed to lighten up and try to have more fun."

"I can't help it that I have a bad back," she said. "I can't run and jump around like he can and like you can. If I do, I spend the next week barely able to sleep; the pain is so bad. I decided it was probably just all in my head, and I couldn't figure out how to compete anyway, other than keep being who I am. So, I put my head in the sand and hoped it would all go away. But it didn't, and now he's gone, and I'll never be able to live without him . . ." She went to her bedroom and slammed the door. I heard wailing and crying and other sounds of her breaking heart.

I tried to console her, and I would like to write that, from then on, I treated my mother with deep empathy and kindness and rallied to her side as a friend and a mature daughter. But that would be a lie. I was angry with them both. Why couldn't everything just be the way it had always been? Why were they ruining my senior year in high school? Why couldn't she be more of whatever it was he wanted? As a teen, I also got frustrated with Mom's cautiousness and had contempt for what I saw as her unadventurous nature and timidity. Sadly, I could imagine feeling just like my dad. I didn't say it to her, and I hated myself for feeling that way, but I doubt I hid it well. That's how awful I was.

Dad called to talk to me now and then and made sure Mom had access to all the money needed to pay the bills, get groceries, and such, but we did not see or hear from him too much the first few weeks after he moved into a rented furnished apartment. My mother and I existed in a fog, numb while also in pain. Mom went to work; I drove myself to school and eventually confided in my girlfriends. I wanted to spend all my time with them, but I needed to be home to share meals with Mom also, though she didn't demand that I do so. She was lonely, but she was determined not to have the disruption interfere with my social life and my happiness. This was my mother in a nutshell—my well-being before hers, always.

I felt so sorry for her, and loved her, and hated that she seemed so vulnerable. I saw how her feelings of helplessness and weakness made her less attractive, which shook her confidence further—a downward spiral. I fussed at her to stand up, get a spine, be strong, put on makeup, and go to the beauty shop. I vowed to never, ever, be weak like her or feel that dependent on a man's affections. I was so naïve.

After a few weeks, Dad called for more than just a quick check-in. I heard Mom's voice warm up and might have even heard her laugh. He told her he missed us and asked if he could come over and visit. When he showed up at the house, holding a pillowcase filled with his dirty clothes, we were both standing there brimming with enough emotions to fill an ocean.

"Hi, you two!" he said smiling. "Thanks a lot for letting me wash clothes here. The laundromat is a real pain!" he said, walking back to the kitchen. "So, how do you use this thing, anyway?" he asked, befuddled by the machine he had walked past daily for more than a decade.

"Oh, move over, and let me take care of it," Mom said, and just like that, she was back to doing his laundry.

"Dad, do you want me to fix you a plate of leftover enchiladas? Mom made them last night," I said. "And she made a pot of pinto beans too." Mom was a great cook, and I knew they were among his many favorites. Who was pathetically trying to please him now?

"Anything need fixing while I'm here? How are you guys doing? Do you need anything?" he asked, with a shy smile.

He stayed longer than he planned. When I left for our high school football game, they were still talking and both had genuine smiles on their faces. He came over again later in the week and for dinner the next week. They talked, he flirted, and she accepted his hang-dog apologies with embarrassing eagerness. I was angry at my father for thinking he could just waltz back into our lives, but just like her, I was overwhelmed with thanks that he might be coming home and swallowed my pride. I was angry at myself for letting him off the hook so easily, but I turned that anger into my existing teenage contempt for my mother, I am ashamed to say, and once again vowed never to be so infatuated by a man. Dad was back home by Christmas.

I had so enjoyed being the confident, bold high school senior, dating different guys and thinking about going to college with my friends. But that girl had gone in hiding when my dad left home, and she wasn't coming out any time soon. I could not bear the insecurities inherent in dating boys I barely knew, watching Mom and Dad, worried that they would split again. Of course, I called Jeff and told him all about my family's saga, and he was there for me, adoring and warm and solid. Against my better judgment, I agreed to go steady with him again, and by early 1970, we decided to marry. I remember giving myself stern lectures about why this made sense.

Jeff and I had a lot in common, including the church and our youth group friends, and we spent hours upon hours having intense, passionate conversations about good and evil, right and wrong, and what our futures might look like. Plus, we were very physically attracted to each other. We had grown up together and were best friends in so many ways. It must be what God wanted, and I was just being rebellious to consider anything else, right? We were perfect for each other, and besides, I could not imagine ever being comfortable enough to be sexually intimate with another person. Didn't the Apostle Paul say, "Better to marry than to burn"? I was about to go up in flames, so another good reason to get married. But I was also a bit sad about what I might be giving up.

Photo 3: Jeff and I after we got back together and planned to marry, 1969 or 1970.

Jeff and I wanted to marry immediately after my high school graduation, but since I would still only be seventeen years old, we needed my parents to consent. They were not enthusiastic but eventually agreed to it if Jeff agreed to put his college plans on hold and support us until I finished my college degree. He had finished three semesters of core college courses, and he was more than ready to take a break, especially since the military draft lottery had just taken place for the first time and his number—298 out of 365—was such that he was probably safe from being drafted to Vietnam. Jeff quit school and got a job working for Southwestern Bell Telephone in an entry level position in the mail room. He applied for every hands-on outdoor position available, and after four to six months, he advanced to a repairman position, and about a month before we wed, he had his own repair van from which he worked.

My mother and her best friend, Ruth, got busy sewing a beautiful white beaded, lace-covered satin wedding dress with a train and veil. Bridesmaids and best men were selected, flowers and color schemes decided upon, and my mother and I, along with all the important women in my orbit, planned our wedding. Friends and family gave us showers and parties, and we talked about how exciting it was to be starting our nearly adult lives—college, marriage, independence.

Photo 4: My parents, Fred and Edith, on my right; Jeff's mother and father, Malvis and Walter, on his left. My mother and her best friend, Ruth, sewed my wedding dress and train.

We married at the Highland Hills Church of Christ in July after my high school graduation in 1970. My father had tears in his eyes as he handed me over to Jeff at the altar. The preacher, Ted, whom we looked up to at the time, performed the ceremony, and we had a reception in the church activities room. After the ceremony, Jeff and I stayed one night in a small motel before moving into an upstairs garage apartment with no air conditioning, which, during July and August in south Texas, was hotter than hell. We were already naturals when it came to pleasuring each other but were technically virgins when we married. A month before our wedding, I started birth control pills as it seemed most young married women my age did, being way more convenient than the diaphragms and condoms of our parents' generation. We were happy to be done with holding back our natural instincts to explore and enjoy each other. Jeff, driving his own telephone repair truck by now, typically arranged to be in the vicinity of our apartment when it was time for his lunch hour, and we would slip and slide with the sweat of our lovemaking before he would jump up and shower and then eat his sandwich in the van on the way back to work.

Nights we spent talking, laughing, playing music, and relishing being independent and able to go and do whatever we wanted. We made love most nights, and after, we would talk for hours in bed until we finally reminded ourselves Jeff had to get up for work the next morning. What did we talk about? Philosophical quandaries; our dream future on a farm, living off the land; my college courses; books we were reading; news events—anything and everything. Talking was how we grew individually and how we cemented our bond. Fortunately, by the end of August, we were approved for a modern air-conditioned subsidized apartment in a complex across from Brooks Air Force Base, ten minutes from our parents, where we lived for the next one to two years.

Once Jeff and I married, we lived on a very tight budget. I kept cash in envelopes in the dresser drawer for our bills and groceries and made our lunches for school and work. I started learning how to cook, asking Mom, friends, and church people for recipes and advice, though offers to take meals with our parents were welcomed! The kitchen looked like a tornado had hit it after I attempted things like Boston Cream pie, and many a night the dishes sat in the sink until the next morning. What a mess!

My first married-lady cooked meal for Mom and Dad was lasagna, which I made using the recipe I had gotten from my new friend Jane, of Chicago Italian heritage, who lived upstairs from us in our new apartment. Lasagna was not part of my mother's repertoire—she was more spaghetti and meatballs or other "American" or "Tex-Mex" food—and I was proud to show off an expanded repertoire. I noticed we were becoming closer the longer we lived apart. She seemed a lot smarter than she had been when I was a teen living at home. Funny how that works.

"How long did you boil the lasagna noodles before putting the cheese and sauce on them, honey?" Mom asked after her first surprisingly crunchy bite.

"Boil the noodles?" I asked, wide-eyed, as I bit into my own first brittle lasagna pasta. A moment later, we all burst out laughing. Jane had not realized the level of inexperience she was dealing with when she failed to spell out "First, boil the lasagna noodles" on the recipe card!

Eventually the renters in my parents' first home, where I lived from birth until age five, moved out, and my parents invited us to move in for the same rent we were paying at the apartment—quite a nice deal for a home with a yard and garage. Now we had a washer and dryer of our own and a garage where Jeff could putter around, working on his white '57 Chevy, and Mom and Dad enjoyed being back in their original house whenever they came over to visit. Jeff still planned to go to college to major in forestry after I graduated, but for the time being, he liked having a paycheck and not taking exams.

Meanwhile, I had started college at San Antonio Junior College right after high school graduation, like many of my high school friends and cousins. It was an economical first step while figuring out our career paths. My first semester's freshman biology class had me leaning toward a science degree. The city did not have a public four-year college at that time, and with Jeff having a good job with Ma Bell, I never questioned the idea of staying tethered to San Antonio. So, my choices after exhausting San Antonio Junior College, which I did in eighteen months, were either Trinity University or one of the Catholic schools. I eventually decided to pursue a degree in medical technology. I did not know anyone who had such a job but found it described in a career book in the library and thought it sounded more interesting than being a nurse or teacher, which were the only female role models I had. It was also a degree that was available as a career path at Incarnate Word College, a four-year college option in San Antonio. We were on our way as a young couple: Jeff working for

Southwestern Bell (Ma Bell), me full time in school. I had my own nest now, and I was in control. Or so I thought.

Jeff and I enjoyed evolving into the young adult set of the Highland Hills Church of Christ community after we married. We attended many youth-group events, and Jeff worked with Bill, the youth group leader, as an assistant, befriending the younger guys and girls in a big-brother way while helping with camping and hunting trips. I taught Bible school to little kids, with Glenda, the mother of a church and school friend, Charlie. I loved Glenda, and we made Bible stories come to life, especially the dramatic Old Testament stories, with amazing clothes-pin "people" and "animals," enacting huge battles and events like when Moses saw the unconsumed burning bush, which we recreated using alcohol on cotton balls stuffed into a plastic "bush" that we set on fire!

But I was already proving to be a real pain in the butt for the church establishment, questioning things that many in our church took at face value. I couldn't help calling out inconsistencies or bizarre Biblical messages when I saw them. I remember recounting one such conundrum to Jeff one Sunday after arriving home.

"I just taught our third-grade Sunday school class," I said, "about how God told Abraham to take his son up to an altar and offer him as a sacrifice. And Abraham *did it*! He tied Isaac, his only son, to the altar. He raised his knife and was prepared to murder him!" I said, in a lather. "As I was teaching the lesson, I saw in the kids' eyes how crazy this sounded, and scary! How is this not child abuse, *insanity*? Is this what we teach as a good model for parenting? Did Isaac have access to psychotherapy after that?" Jeff tried to placate me with words about how things were different back then and it was a story of faith and such. I vowed to avoid that Bible story in the future.

Mostly my comments elicited condescending pats on the head from the church adults, but they looked askance at some of my actions. For example, to their shock, and despite Jeff's attempt at shaming me about it, I enthusiastically stood in line in the early 1970s when a performance of the latest sensational rock opera *Jesus Christ Superstar* came to San Antonio.

"You're putting yourself in the hands of Satan by watching this blasphemy!" members of local Christian churches said to us while I waited in line with my high school girlfriend, Danna, to get into the venue. "If you want to know about Jesus and God, read the Bible!" they told us.

"How do you know what they're saying if you haven't even seen it?" I asked. "My faith in God and Christ is strong enough to be open minded and look at things other than the Bible. How about yours?"

Once I saw the musical, I thought it raised some legitimate questions about how Jesus saw Himself and His mission in life (and death) and the idea that the whole thing—Him dying for our sins, as supposedly prophesied in the Old Testament—could not have happened unless Judas Iscariot played his pivotal role by betraying Jesus to the Romans.

"Wasn't Judas just doing God's will?" I asked our Sunday school class one morning. "And if so, why was he cursed? How do we know, and who are we to judge? Or if God did condemn him to hell for playing his part, is that not incredibly hypocritical? And is it not ridiculous, when you think of it, that an omnipotent being 'must' send his beloved son to take on the misery of being a human and then die for our sins? He made evil as well as good, right? He set up the whole scene, the problem, and the answer." Though I loved my church friends and loved the idea of Jesus and God, some of the details did not make much sense when you got right down to it. And "just have faith" wore thin.

Another major sticking point for me was the unfairness that people in distant countries, who had not heard about the Church of Christ's version of Christianity, were supposedly going to burn in hell because they weren't our kind of Christians. I remember being told there was an "out," such that if a person had never heard "the Word," aka the Church of Christ version of truth, God would (probably) have mercy on their souls. But at the same time, we were told, this was why it was so important to support the missionaries so everyone in the world could hear "the Word"! So, then my next thought was, *Wouldn't it be better just never to allow them to hear it? Then there is no chance for hell, right?*

This type of thinking was problematic for a member of a fundamentalist church like the Church of Christ, but I was young and naïve and had no idea of the history of religious bodies or doctrines. While the Catholics had eventually come to realize that they were better off keeping their questioners and seekers close, if possible (i.e., the Jesuits), the fundamentalists were trying to make sure their parishioners toed the line. The Church of Christ followers in our church even believed Baptists were going to hell, even though they are exceedingly close to one another in almost all their beliefs including things that set them aside from Catholicism, like total immersion for baptism, baptism as a choice (once an age of reason is reached rather than as an infant), and Bible *pro scripta*. The fact that my best friend Laurie and her family, who lifted their voices in praise to the accompaniment of a musical instrument and were supposedly going to hell for this technicality, seemed ludicrous. Couldn't we just all agree on the big stuff—God's love, Jesus in the manger loving the little children, the Ten Commandments, being kind—and let the little stuff go?

CHAPTER 4:

HERETICS

Summer and Fall 1973

While Jeff and I were getting on with our married lives in San Antonio, we enjoyed occasional visits with our friend Charlie who had moved away after high school to attend Abilene Christian College, a Church of Christ-affiliated school. When we saw him during school breaks, it was obvious that he also was changing, growing into himself, and seeing the world in his own unique way. He looked less and less like the clean-cut model of a preacher-to-be and more typical of a young person of the times, with longer hair and, eventually, a full dark beard. One early summer evening he came to our house for supper.

Jeff broached a topic that had been bothering us a great deal in the past few weeks.

"So, Charlie," Jeff said, "Bill has asked me to be his assistant with the youth group at church, and Susie and I were invited to the preacher's house a couple weeks ago as part of the leadership group. You know what they talked about the whole time? The attendance numbers at church on Sunday and what the collection plate figures were like!" Charlie nodded his head, unsurprised. Jeff continued. "It seems like the more we get to know about how things work at church, the more we see that it's about the dollars and keeping the preacher paid."

"Yeah, I know what you mean," Charlie said. "You know my dad is one of the elders, so he also goes to those meetings and it's all they seem to talk about. I told him I thought it was absurd that a church has any savings at all! They should be permanently bankrupt because they are spending every penny to feed and house the poor. He asked how we would pay the preacher, and I said we should all be preachers while doing a normal job. That's what Jesus did! That's what we all should be doing! We shouldn't pay preachers at all."

I discovered that I had much in common with Charlie, including what I saw as the disconnect between the radical ideas that Jesus espoused and the judgmental status quo that our church seemed intent on focusing on. Jeff started to lean toward my point of view.

"My parents don't know it, but I've gotten to where I almost never go to the college Church of Christ anymore. Instead, a group of my friends and I meet at someone's place and pray and sing and then go take food to someone or help fix someone's house in the area. And I've been writing songs about Jesus and God's love, and I don't believe I'm sinning because I'm singing the words to the accompaniment of my guitar!" he confessed. This was a surprise since I always thought Charlie was destined to be a Church of Christ preacher or some other church official. "I'm finding more joy in God now than I ever have in church, and I no longer believe that only the Church of Christ has the answers or the keys to heaven."

We agreed to keep meeting together and studying the Bible in this new light while Charlie was in town for the summer. We started inviting others in our church's congregation who seemed of like mind, mostly people our age, to study with us, and the enthusiasm and intensity of our beliefs blossomed. Jeff, who was raised in the Church of Christ and not a rabble-rouser by nature, was tentative at first; it seemed heretical and threatening. I pushed him to consider these more inclusive ideas, and he was eventually willing to listen, though it put him at loggerheads with the traditional beliefs he had grown up with.

Photo 5: Jeff and I as a young married couple, enjoying Christmas with my parents and family friends Ruth (to Dad's right) and Jim who was taking the picture.

Meanwhile, there were other changes at home. Jeff applied for and eventually attained a lineman training position, and he was proud of that. This was a great promotion and put him on track for a secure, well-paying job. But the new job also put him in the company of men who were older, of a generation we had previously thought of as the dads and uncles of the world, not college educated, and of a rougher sort than I was used to, for sure. He came home telling tales reflecting their language, points of view, prejudices, and a new kind of peer pressure.

"Guthrie said if the 'women's libbers' have their way, soon there'll be a law making us hire girls as linemen. I told him you would agree with how ridiculous that was, even though you are kind of a 'women's libber,'" Jeff said one night at the dinner table.

"I am not a women's libber," I said. Though I adamantly believed girls should be allowed to pursue any career they chose, I did not yet embrace the movement or the label. "But what's so ridiculous about hiring a girl to learn to be a lineman? I know girls who loved to climb stuff growing up. I bet they could learn to climb a telephone poll just like you," I said.

"Maybe, but what about lifting the transformers and puttin' the poles up and carrying the creosote? Girls can't lift stuff that heavy!" he said.

"But y'all work as a team, so if something is too heavy, you lift it together or get a tool or machine to help, right? I doubt any one of you is putting telephone poles up all by yourselves anyway. Plus, you could divide up the labor, so if it's too heavy, a man could do that part, and something that needs more nimble fingers the girls could do. Plus, I bet lots of girls would rather make the pay of a lineman than the money they get paid as a secretary," I said.

"But what if they had to go the bathroom or something? We just go over in the bushes and take a piss or do our business. What would a girl do? And if she went into the bushes, all the guys would be thinking about what she was doing in there and, well, you know . . ." he trailed off, confident he had made the defining case against women in a man's working world.

"Wait, that's Guthrie talking, right?" I said. "Jeff, we go camping all the time with family and even church friends, and you've seen me, or other girls, disappear into the bushes to do our business if there is no toilet around. You never told me you thought that was weird or unladylike. Did we cause all the boys to start lusting in their hearts because we went somewhere to squat and pee? Really?" I asked.

He also started using language and telling jokes that disparaged blacks and Hispanics, invoking centuries-old stereotypes, viewpoints I had never heard him espouse before. I hated it when he talked that way and called him on it. I had started to embrace the idea of affirmative action, realizing it was an important long-term investment to reverse centuries of systemic racism and prejudice, giving the trod-upon a leg up in the workforce. However, this was a hard argument for me too. I had seen the hurt and anger in my dad when he was passed over for promotion at Kelly Air Force Base despite higher test scores, hard work, and commendations because they had embarked on an affirmative action strategy. In school, I was learning about Brown vs the Board of Education and the exclusionary power of "good ol' boys" networks, while Jeff was learning about how threatened blue-collar working men felt by both women and minorities. We were learning the facts of life as adults and diverging in our opinions.

In the winter of 1972, after I transferred from San Antonio Junior college to Incarnate Word College (now University) to pursue a degree in medical technology, Jeff got sick with hepatitis A, otherwise known as "yellow jaundice." This type of liver infection is caused by a virus spread via the fecal-oral route, meaning that someone sick with the disease can carry the virus on their hands and accidentally contaminate surfaces or the food that others eat. Sick restaurant workers, for example, can be the source of a community outbreak of hepatitis A. We never figured out where Jeff got infected, but he was quite sick; he had no appetite and lost weight. He had very little energy, was jaundiced, had night sweats, and stayed feverish for weeks. He had to stay home from work, church, and away from friends and family, other than me, for about six weeks, sleeping and resting for hours every day.

One evening during his illness, I came home from church, and he told me he awoke from a nap to the vision of an angel there in the bedroom with him. If the angel spoke, Jeff did not remember what it said, but Jeff took it as a signal that our Bible studies were a good thing, and we were on the right path toward serving God. He was no longer hesitant to embrace a more open, loving, and nonconformist attitude toward Christianity and reading the Bible with open eyes, focused less on damnation and more on love.

At the same time, my college required twelve semester hours of philosophy or religion, and I took an intersession three-week course where we studied and visited ten or more different churches, synagogues, and temples of various world religions: Christian (Roman and Greek Catholic, black Baptist, Presbyterian, and Lutheran), Jewish, Muslim, and Baha'i faith, to name a few. All were sincere, and all had common rules—do not murder, lie, steal, fornicate and be kind to each other—and then smaller things that made them unique. I marveled that it was the small unique, seemingly trivial things that each one seemed to hold most dear. My experiences and observations led to even more spirited group discussion among our growing Bible study group.

We unintentionally developed a following of twenty to thirty like-minded young adults from the Highland Hills Church of Christ, who came to our house regularly for Bible study and lively discussions. We were not alone. The counter-culture hippie movement in the US also spawned "Jesus people" or "Jesus freaks" who also tended to be anti-war and distrustful of the establishment, though not focused on sex, drugs, and rock-and-roll espoused by the original flower child movement. In fact, *Time* magazine featured the *Jesus Revolution* on their cover in June 1971. An ecumenical movement emerged in mainstream churches, and some congregations sought greater unity and cross-collaboration in their communities. Some even offered more expressive "charismatic" and evangelical worship where people "spoke in tongues." We were influenced by evangelical books and started sprinkling phrases like "praise Jesus" and "praise God" throughout our speech.

"Good morning, Susie Green," Deacon Smith might say. "What a beautiful spring day! Good to see you at church this fine morning. Is Jeff here?"

"Praise the Lord, Mr. Smith," I said. "It's all to His glory. Yes, Jeff's already gone inside, and I'm off to Mr. Carlyle's class. Have a blessed day!" Deacon Smith would have done a double take at my new way of speaking and wondered where I was getting it from. These days I see the language reflected in the television adaptation of Margaret Atwood's book *The Handmaid's Tale*.

We increasingly felt that we were on to something qualitatively different than what our Church of Christ brethren were focused on but sincerely believed that, as soon as they understood about this new joyful approach to Christianity, focused on loving one another and not damning one another, they would join the lovefest. I still enjoy thinking about our earnest, innocent young selves. The hammer had yet to fall.

I had not considered churches as self-protective institutions or religious belief as a tool for tribal or societal manipulation and control, so I was blindsided by the unfolding events. The leadership at the Highland Hills Church of Christ where we worshipped acted predictably, in many ways. They were confident that they had the correct interpretation of God's wishes and saw themselves as good shepherds, admonishing their members to follow the rules to avoid God's wrath, in this life or the hereafter. They knew that their institution, the church, needed stability—financial and social—so they could keep their members safe from sin and depredation, so it was their job to maintain the status quo. Imagine if people were allowed to think independently? The flood gates would open, and a plethora of new religions would arise, less perfect than theirs but diminishing their power, nonetheless. They were right.

In mid-summer 1973, while Charlie was at home on break from college, our Bible study group and unorthodox ideas gained the attention of the preacher who began lobbying the most senior church leaders, the church elders, to take action to stop our activities. Jeff and I were separately called in to face the preacher and the elders, as was Charlie. They set themselves up in the church activities room and questioned us one by one. I knew these men; they had been like dads and uncles to me since I was a kid. They seemed almost as uncomfortable as I was during the interrogation.

"Susie," the first elder said, "we've gotten reports that a Bible study group has been meeting at your house, and we're worried that you don't understand how dangerous it might be. Can you tell us what you believe and what you and your husband and friends are teaching?"

"I'm not teaching anything," I said. "We come together and pray that the Lord will open our minds to his Word, and then one of us randomly picks a passage from the New Testament of the Bible and someone reads it, and we try to listen to the words as though we'd never heard them before. We ask the Lord to enlighten our hearts to their meaning. We try to focus on Jesus's words as much as possible. What we've learned, and what is amazing, is that we almost always find a passage about helping the poor and sick, about not holding on to earthly riches and possessions, and about sharing what we have, about loving and respecting each other. We have read the verses that supposedly say that someone is going to hell because they weren't baptized exactly right or sing alongside a piano or guitar, and . . . they are vague, at best."

"Susie, what is your goal?" the second elder asked. "Are you trying to start your own church? Are there other churches or other preachers you've heard, or know, who you're following? Give us their names so we can find out their motives."

"No, sir," I said. "There's no one like that. We started thinking about things when we got turned off by how much focus there is on collection plate amounts rather than on doing the Lord's work. And then Charlie told us there are others around the country and at Abilene Christian College who are also thinking like this, and we've read books about other churches taking a more open and accepting approach to Christianity. We just started praying and thinking, I guess. It's just us." I looked at them and then added, "And God. Us and God, through our prayers. Praise the Lord."

"Susie," said a third elder, "we want you and Jeff and Charlie to stop these so-called Bible studies. Stick with Sunday school. It's confusing to young people who look up to you, and it's a slippery slope. We believe what you are teaching is blasphemous. If you won't stop, we may need to consider disfellowshipping you all, for your own good and for the good of the congregation. Will you stop?"

"But wait, you can't mean it! We're just reading the Bible together, and it says a lot about more about love and acceptance than damning everybody to hell. You would disfellowship us for that?"

"Will you stop?"

"I'll pray about it," I said, and I left.

I was dumbfounded. I was embarrassed, and then I felt anger at being shamed for finding joy and love in the teachings of Jesus Christ. It dawned on me that the preacher, Ted, had sat in the back of the room and never said a word, though I was sure he was the one most upset about our Bible study group. He was having the elders and deacons do his dirty work. They were unwise not to see that we were idealistic and naïve but not likely to foment full-on rebellion.

Jeff and Charlie had similar interviews and were given the same message: cease and desist, or be rejected from the church. We described our ordeal when our Bible study group met again and prayed about it. The group supported us in whatever we thought best. They did not want to put us in a bad position, but they were incensed by how we were being treated, how we were all being treated, like wayward children, not sincere, thoughtful members of the church community. We decided we needed to keep on doing what we were doing: meeting, reading, and praying and looking for ways to serve others.

Biblical precedent for disfellowshipment is sparse, but the verse that probably comes the closest was written by the Apostle Paul in a letter to an early Corinthian Christian church when he wrote, 1 Corinthians 5: 9-11: "I wrote you in my letter not to associate with immoral people; I did not at all mean with the immoral people of this world, or with the covetous and swindlers, or with idolaters, for then you would have to go out of the world. But actually, I wrote to you not to associate with any so-called brother if he is an immoral person, or covetous, or an idolater, or a reviler, or a drunkard, or a swindler[—]not even to eat with such a one." Or this one from 2 Thessalonians 3:14: "If anyone does not obey our instruction in this letter, take special note of that person and do not associate with him, so that he will be put to shame." Since Charlie, Jeff, and I were not immoral (e.g., not murderers, adulterers, thieves), covetous, idolators (worshiping Baal? Ashur?), revilers (of what?), drunkards, or swindlers, we could not understand on what basis they could possibly disfellowship us. We kept praying.

What happened next seemed overly dramatic in response to our simple Bible study group. Charlie remembers it as something "right out of a movie."

Our telephone rang one Saturday, and Charlie was on the line.

"Jeff, get Susie. We need to talk." Jeff found me, and we huddled around the phone receiver. "We're here, Charlie. What's up?" he said.

"My dad got a call from Ted, who is not going to let this go. He is demanding that the elders disfellowship us. They don't really want to, but he is threatening to resign if they don't. He wants my dad to be the one to do the disfellowship service, but Dad refuses. I think we are going to get an official letter soon, and it will give a date when it happens," said Charlie. His father was a highly respected elder and music director. I did not know the half of the intense pressure the preacher was using to force the issue. Years later, I learned the rest of the story.

"Ted called Dad one evening," Charlie told me recently, "and said that we had to be stopped and disfellowshipment was the only way. He said he had the support of the other elders, but he specifically wanted my dad to perform the disfellowship service, like that would make it more legitimate. He said that, if my dad agreed to do the service, he would make sure that only you and Jeff would be disfellowshipped. But if Dad refused, I would be included in the disfellowship proceedings, also. Of course, Dad refused, and that's why it was all three of us. Can you believe it? Extortion!" Charlie said. "He swore me to secrecy because he didn't want to be the one to spread rumors. It was a terrible position to put my dad in. Ted was a mean little man."

Indeed, the preacher drafted certified letters and got enough elders to sign them so he could consider it legitimate and sent them to Jeff and me as a couple and to Charlie separately. The letters stated the date and time of the service and demanded that we repent before or during the service or be banished from the community. At the ages of twenty-one and twenty-three, studying the Bible and trying to live what we understood as Jesus Christ's teachings to love and serve our fellow man, we were going to be drummed out of our own church. It seemed outrageous and senseless.

As the day drew near, we discussed how to approach the event: go to the service, or shun it altogether.

"I am not ashamed of our beliefs or the fact that others want to come to our house to pray and talk about Jesus Christ!" I proclaimed, to nods and "amens" from Jeff and Charlie.

"We need to go to the service," Charlie said, "so they are forced to see us and recognize we are the same as we've always been. We're not bad or evil, and we don't feel guilty. Also, I want the preacher and the elders to realize the weight and gravity of what they are doing to the congregation, not just to us."

"I grew up with them! They're like family!" Jeff said. "We've loved them, and they have loved us for years. They need to feel what they are doing to their own kin. But, man, it's going to be a long service. I am not looking forward to this."

"We're going to be praying and saying, 'Praise Jesus,' the whole time!" said Charlie with a full-on smile on his face.

My parents thought the entire thing was ridiculous and counseled us to change churches. Jeff's and Charlie's parents both asked us to reconsider.

"Just come back to church, study more quietly, apologize just a little, and let the whole thing calm down," was their advice. But we were resolute, and as an act of principle, we attended the service and, in so doing, endured an uncomfortable and heartbreaking hour in the spotlight.

It was the end of summer, and though the church was air conditioned, it was hot and muggy, and the pews were packed. Charlie, Jeff, and I sat about a third of the way toward the front, along the aisle on the left, facing the preacher. We sat together, with friends, family, and supporters in front and behind us in pews. Ted was trying to look calm, but his prominent Adam's apple bobbed frequently against his necktie and his pale blue eyes were red-rimmed and sadder than usual. He was clearly unsettled by the fact that he would not be preaching about a theoretical source of idolatrous influence but preaching in the presence of our innocent young faces. I suspect he had hoped we would not call his bluff, but we did. Would his flock believe that we were somehow evil and needed to be expelled?

I do not remember exactly what Ted said, but I know he impugned the sincerity and value of our beliefs and negated the goodness of our intentions. It seemed to go on forever, and we were too intimidated to get up and argue. No one else stood and spoke up in our defense, either, though many were so disgusted that, once it was over, they never darkened the congregation's doorways again. Jeff looked grim and uncomfortable. Charlie tried smiling and seemed to be muttering prayers to keep his spirits up. We held hands. Charlie remembers that Ted focused on the 1 Corinthians verse about immoral acts, as though we were having orgies at our house instead of Bible studies. Finally, the preacher stopped preaching and demanded that we come to the front of the church, repent, and ask forgiveness or be unwelcome in the church, unwelcome at our church friends' and families' tables, and shunned by the congregation. Clocks ticked and the minutes passed while we sat there silent, our heads held high. We were sad and grieving for them and perhaps for our lost innocence, but unrepentant. Finally, the long silence was broken by a closing hymn that I believe Charlie's father led, putting everyone out of their misery. The congregation stayed seated, not sure what to do, and we stepped out from the pew, walked down the aisle holding hands, and out the church doors.

CHAPTER 5

JESUS FREAKS

Fall 1973, On the Road, Texas to California

We kept praying and Bible studies continued at our house, but we felt a shift in our lives. Jeff's career as a lineman for Southwestern Bell Telephone Company was going well, but I was at a crossroads with school. I had finished classwork and had started the final practicum year to become a medical technologist at Bexar County Hospital, the teaching hospital affiliated with the University of Texas Health Science Center. Rotations through the hospital's clinical laboratory were a window to the career I had chosen, and before long I realized I was not enjoying it.

I had thought a career in medical technology (med tech) was a good fit because all the pre-clinical coursework included things I was interested in such as microbiology, parasitology, and embryology. But at the hospital we had almost no interaction with the doctors or patients, and other than in blood banking and the microbiology part of the laboratory, we were mainly caretakers of laboratory equipment and quality control. However, I treasured the early-morning part-time job I took as a phlebotomist, going throughout the hospital with blood-drawing equipment and slips of paper stating the patient's name and bed number, the type of blood tests needed for the day, and potential diagnoses. This gave me an opportunity to interact with patients and connect the lab tests with the person and their medical problems. As sleepy as they were, I relished our brief interactions and tried to make my visit as painless for them as possible. I looked forward to seeing their progress every morning, but the rest of the day was pure boredom from my point of view.

The long morning commute at least was interesting after one of my med tech classmates, Kathy, and I started carpooling together. I knew she was a single mom of two boys, but it was several months before she filled me in on how that came to be. She and her husband met while working as volunteers helping to unionize Latino farmworkers in the fertile farmlands and orchards of south Texas. Their group was trying to do in Texas what Cesar Chavez, the Mexican American civil rights activist, had done in California. They used nonviolent methods to pressure owners to provide better pay and working conditions for the Rio Grande valley farm workers. After their volunteer stint ended, they moved to San Antonio, her husband's hometown, and started a family. She taught school, while he helped his mother with child care for their boys while also doing freelance language translation and support for legal services in the Hispanic community. Unfortunately, once they were away from the constraints of the volunteer organization, it became clear that her husband had a drinking problem. An articulate and intelligent activist, a caring husband and father when sober, he was none of those things when drinking. He was riding in a car with friends one day when they were stopped by police and found to have a stolen TV in the trunk. He pronounced his innocence but was hauled in with the rest of them and sentenced to several years in the Texas state penitentiary in Huntsville. Thus,

Kathy was working on her second college degree to get a better paying job as the sole breadwinner of her family.

While I was struggling to find enjoyment in my career as a med tech, Jeff and I began to envision a life focused on serving God and trying to emulate the teachings of Jesus, especially in the company of like-minded people. Jeff and I were very much in sync with each other in this idea, and we kept coming back to Matthew 19:21: "Jesus said to him, 'If you want to be perfect, go, sell what you have and give to the poor, and you will have treasure in heaven; and come, follow Me.'" After much discussion and prayer, Jeff and I decided to quit job and school, give away or sell all our worldly possessions, leave our families and friends in San Antonio, and move to Abilene to audit classes alongside Charlie and his friends at Abilene Christian College. We wanted to study early church history as well as the Greek language the New Testament was written in, to better understand exactly what Jesus said—not what people had interpreted him to have said and intended. We felt certain we would meet others like us. Charlie was about to start his senior year there and welcomed us to join him. He suggested we find a house large enough for the three of us and perhaps other friends he studied and worshipped with. We gave away almost everything and left our red Plymouth Barracuda with Kathy, happy to know that she had at least one less thing to worry about.

We moved to Abilene, Texas, a town of about ninety thousand, a four-hour drive almost due north of San Antonio in north central Texas, south of Lubbock and Amarillo. What I remember is that it was flat, very, very flat, which was good, because we bought variable speed bicycles when we arrived and that was our only transportation option for school, work, grocery shopping, and socializing. It was hard, humbling, and gratifying.

Those of us who rode bikes to school especially recognized each other on rainy days.

"You too," my classmate said, and I noticed him pointing to the wet stripe up my back and the wet bell-bottom jean cuffs I had just released from their rubber band. He had similar markings on his back and jeans. I was glad to be a compatriot; it made me feel adventurous, edgy, and independent, nothing like the married church lady I had been a few months ago. I was no longer struggling to get up every hill, and I could easily ride the straightaways with no hands, able to stretch my back for a bit. When one of us craved ice cream or decided we must see Franco Zeffirelli's *Brother Sun, Sister Moon*, we had to calculate not just the money needed, but the time and energy required to get ourselves there and back again.

Abilene was home to three major church-affiliated colleges when we were there, all of which have subsequently grown to university status: Abilene Christian College is affiliated with the Churches of Christ, Hardin-Simmons with the Southern Baptist churches, and the smallest, McMurry, is associated with the Methodist churches. As such, the town had a feeling of staidness, propriety, and wholesomeness. Charlie, Jeff, and I pooled our three part-time paychecks and rented a run-down but spacious unfurnished house, and before long we were the focal point for large communal meals, Bible studies, and gospel songfests attended by more than twenty people, including many who had formed a bond with Charlie in his earlier years at school, many of whom almost certainly had a crush on him.

Photo 6: Charlie, senior year of high school

Charlie was classically handsome, confident, and charismatic, while most of his peers were still awkwardly lurching toward adulthood. He could disarm even the most determined curmudgeon with his beaming smile and brown eyes with lashes any girl would envy. When he was in a room, everyone gravitated toward him to hear his thoughts, his banter, and his songs, basking in his presence and attention. He was not particularly tall—about 5'8"—with broad shoulders and a muscular torso and legs thanks to his having worked construction during the summers. During college, he honed his skills at songwriting, mostly focused on either praise of God and Jesus Christ or the hypocrisy of organized religion in their distortion of what he felt was true. He accompanied each song with his guitar and either piano or harmonica held coat-hanger style ala Bob Dylan.

Our classes were very instructive and, like any good institute of higher learning, made us examine preconceived notions and think fresh thoughts. I confirmed what I had learned in religion classes during my Catholic undergraduate studies at Incarnate Word College, that unlike what the Church of Christ preacher told us, the Bible was not handed down *in toto* to us, and the Protestant churches were Johnny-come-lately compared to the centuries of early Christianity embodied in the Catholic church. Further, the texts in the Bible were not written soon after Jesus spoke the Sermon on the Mount, for example, or even a few months later, but decades and decades after Jesus's death. The actual words quoted from Jesus were few and far between, remembered years later, and yes, it is hard to follow the events of his life by reading the four gospels because their writings were not contemporaneous with Jesus's life, nor were they written in a coordinated fashion with one another. And the final decisions about what to include and what to leave out of what we now call the Bible were decided by men approximately five hundred years later. All of this begged the question of why churches seemed to make such a big deal about certain little things they had interpreted from scripture when so much may have already been lost or misinterpreted during language or cultural translation. Having a difference of opinion is one thing, but believing that others will burn in hell because they do not believe in your interpretation of a few passages still made no sense to me.

I am sure there was much else that I learned, but mainly the deeper I dug, the less confidence I had that any church, including the Church of Christ, had all the answers. However, when I tried to ask our professors how they could maintain their faith after knowing all these things, most of them retreated to the "mysteries" of God and how, even with all the human frailties and manipulation, God must have been guiding the process to have created such a perfect document as the Bible. Studying Greek seemed less imperative once I learned that Jesus and his apostles did not speak Greek, the language of the New Testament writings, nor even Hebrew, most likely, but almost certainly Aramaic. The original Greek text is already at least once removed from the primary source.

Despite an interesting group of friends and faculty in Abilene, Jeff, Charlie, and I became more and more convinced that our views and our interest in a fully committed search for a like-minded community were not going to be fulfilled within the confines of the college or the Church of Christ, no matter how open minded the congregation was. Perhaps we would need to look further afield. There was local buzz about a Christian commune that had sprung up about an hour to the east of Abilene. Charlie told us he visited the group the year before and described it to us as an example of where we might find a home. They called themselves the Children of God.

"The people seemed focused on the important things about Jesus Christ's teachings," Charlie said. "Their ideas and teachings resonated. I seriously thought about quitting college and going back there to live with them, but before I could do anything about it, I learned that they moved their entire operation to somewhere in California." We made plans to head west to find the Children of God commune and visit other groups along the way and were confident that God would take care of the details. But how were we going to get there?

Charlie and Jeff advocated for "hopping a freight" as the most efficient way to get to the West Coast and even went to a local train yard to scope out the prospects. They were less enthusiastic once they saw the reality, and I was terrified of the idea. I was certain I would be unable to jump onto the train (weak arms, slow legs) and would be left behind—or even more terrifying, dragged under the train and cut in half by the wheels . . . very graphic fears indeed.

Interestingly, I do not remember that we considered going cross-country by bike; we probably never knew anyone who had embarked on a long ride like that, though now I know that it was a common practice in Europe. In fact, my current husband rode a bike through Europe the summer after high school, ten years earlier. In any event, my refusal to go by train prevailed, and we decided to hitchhike.

Humans with a mode of transportation at their disposal, be it cart and donkey, horse and wagon, car or truck, often share their transportation for a price or for their own altruistic reasons. In the countryside of African and Asian countries, people walking along the road commonly use an up-and-down hand motion to indicate an interest in negotiating a price for a lift toward their destination. Conversely, passing vehicles slow down to inquire if those walking want a ride for some payment. In America and Europe, hitchhiking became common in the early days of motorized vehicle travel during the Great Depression and later when GIs were on furlough after WWII. However, when I was a kid growing up, the only people hitchhiking on the roads looked seedy and all the adults I knew warned of murderers along the highway and assumed they were freeloading "bums and winos." Jack Kerouac's writings gave voice to the Beat Generation that begat our generation either returning from the war in Vietnam or out looking for America and their future selves. So, by the time we were preparing to hit the road in the early 1970s, hitchhiking had become very common again, with people willing to pick up folks who looked safe and simpatico.

As we got more serious about our trip and its planning, a friend of Charlie's named Brad started talking about coming with us. He was part of the Bible study and worship group that met at our house in Abilene, though Jeff and I didn't know him well.

"What's your interest, Brad? I know you're friends with Charlie, but what's your main thing?" Jeff asked him one day.

"I'm a physics major," Brad said, "which makes my parents happy, and I like physics; it's interesting. But I can't imagine doing a physics related job the rest of my life. If I had it my way, I would be a professional musician, playing violin for the symphony. But my parents can't imagine that for me. I've been an A student all my life, and they think a music career would be a waste."

Brad was certain his parents would not agree with the decision to change majors. They also wouldn't be happy if he dropped out of Abilene Christian College and hitchhiked around the country. In fact, it would be the first time he had seriously gone against them in his life. Still, he was very unhappy at school, and he knew that our leaving would deprive him of his companionship with Charlie, one of the few people he considered his intellectual equal. Among ourselves, we had some concerns about having a fourth person in our group. Getting a ride for three people was already going to be challenging, but four? Maybe impossible. On the other hand, four was safer than three, and at least then we could split into pairs instead of having an odd man out. In the end, we agreed, and he decided to cast his lot with us. He also started divesting himself of most of the things he had in his dorm room and steeling himself for the conversation with his parents.

We knew we needed to travel as light as possible because everything would be carried on our backs, but we needed some basic things to stay alive while living rough along the road. We assumed we would spend most nights sleeping outdoors, and this was before the days when super-lightweight camping gear was readily available at specialty stores like Recreational Equipment Inc (REI) co-op. So our backpacks were army surplus green canvas bags and a water-resistant poncho tarp we could use as a lean-to, ground cloth, or rain poncho as needed. We carried Coleman cotton sleeping bags rolled up and put in stuff bags on top of the entire contraption. The pack plus the sleeping bag plus the rain poncho created a heavy, cumbersome burden that was not comfortable for long walks or hikes. We also packed one change of clothes, toiletries, and, of course, a Bible.

The weekend before we left, my mom drove up from San Antonio and stayed with us for two nights. My father had left her a second time, and this time they divorced. In short order, he married a woman named Marie who had a young daughter. Mom continued to support the idea that I should live my life as I saw fit and not worry about her. I do not remember any major disapproval from her, but she could not have been happy that I had dropped out of college and was going to hitchhike around the country.

"Susie, my life is a mess right now," she said while we stayed up late talking one night. "Your dad is off married to that low-life woman, Marie, but I'll survive. He had to pay me for his half of the house, and I have that money in certificates of deposit earning good interest, so I'm OK financially. My boss and friends at work think I'm wonderful, I have your Aunt Louise and Uncle Don to talk to and do stuff with, plus our sorority group has plenty of projects that I'm going to get busy with. You need to live your life the way you want to live it and not sit around worrying about me," she said and then turned to Jeff.

"But you, young man, better keep my daughter safe, you hear me! I mean it!" she said, as tears finally sprang to her eyes and mine. We hugged and cried, and she gave me a roll of dimes to make sure I would call home on any pay phone I found along the way. I look back and wonder how I could have been so callous to leave her alone in San Antonio. Was I really that oblivious to her pain and loneliness? I burned with such a passionate intensity for *my* life that I was certain she would support me—which she did.

Photo 7: My mother and I, circa 1972

We gave notice to our landlord, let our professors know we were leaving, said goodbye to our friends, and quit our part-time jobs: me at a local burger joint, Jeff and Charlie working in the college cafeteria. We had saved a decent amount of money and took most of it to the bursar's office and at Charlie's suggestion had them apply it to the account of one of the Bible study group members who Charlie was convinced had school debt that was crushing him and his elderly parents.

We headed west, talking to other hitchhikers and people who gave us rides along the way, sharing our beliefs and quest, and started accepting the popular moniker of the day of being "Jesus freaks" as it described us more accurately than the other stereotype of free love, drugs-seeking hippies. Quite the opposite, we did not smoke pot or do drugs and drank little, if any, alcohol partly because we had very little money and partly because we were still more or less living as though we were following the rules and regulations of the Church of Christ where drugs and alcohol are discouraged.

Our focus was spiritual, and we were determined to find a place where we belonged.

It quickly became obvious that the interstate highway system was the best place to get a ride. Smaller roads were less well travelled and had fewer people willing to pick us up. Since there were four of us, we constantly made plans for where to meet if we got split up since we thought it unlikely that we would always get a ride as a foursome, but in fact, often we did get a ride together, especially in the back of a truck or a van. Several people told us that the fact there was a girl with us made them more likely to pick us up— no female axe murderers?—and Charlie's guitar slung over his bag made a good impression as well. We usually made sure Charlie sat up front as he was the most comfortable engaging with strangers and seemed to be able to talk to most anyone. We paid attention, however, for signs of danger or drivers who might be unhinged.

One ride I remember was with several young men in a truck being driven by a guy in his twenties who told us that he was on his first big cross-country trip, with friends, since coming out of a six-month coma after an accident. His friends corroborated his story, and he seemed no worse for the wear as far as we could tell. We were picked up by both men and women, several of whom took us to their communal living situations where we helped with the cooking and clean-up while sharing meals, a roof over our heads for a night's rest, and breakfast in the morning. Often Charlie would sing songs he had written or songs popular on the radio, and everyone would sing along.

There were very few times that I felt unsafe during the actual hitchhiking part of the journey, though I was careful to stay close to my husband and two other healthy, strong young male traveling companions. One time we arranged to be let off at a rest stop as we parted ways with a driver about to deviate from our westward heading, and I walked up to the toilets by myself, leaving my backpack with my companions on the interstate.

"Hey there, I'm headed west. How about you? I'm happy to give you a ride!" said the middle-aged driver of a semi-tractor-trailer truck that had pulled alongside me as I approached the rest area. He was smiling and seemed very friendly. We had been surprised to have gotten few offers from the big-rig drivers up to that point, so this seemed like good news.

"Yes, let me go get my friends!" I said.

"Oh no, honey, just you, is all," he replied, hoping his smile was even more charming.

"*Oh!* Right! Um, no thanks, my *husband* waiting for me on the interstate would not be very happy about that!" I said trying to keep the flutters out of my voice and walking more quickly to cut across the grassy patch to the girls' bathroom. That was a wake-up call, and I was happy to return to the safety of my group.

Another time we attempted to set up camp along the highway before noticing a group of older more hardcore "real" homeless men already there. They got testy with us.

"You hippies! Just of bunch of draft dodgers! Taking your mommy and daddy's money and havin' the time of your lives, yeah. Smokin' pot, gettin' easy rides cause you look like rich white kids while the rest of us are actually hungry out here," one of them said.

"It ain't no choice for me, not since my daddy kicked me outta the house when I was fifteen," said another. "I been livin' out here ever since, no one but me to count on!" he spat out, successfully making me feel threatened and guilty at the same time. The incident brought into focus the fact that we had chosen this adventure; we were not experiencing generations-long bone-deep poverty. We were "living rough," which sometimes meant going without food, because we had chosen to do so. We knew their criticisms and resentments were not much off the mark. We were not watching our children go hungry, struggling each month to pay rent, or being threatened with eviction from our house. While there was danger on the road, it was danger we had put ourselves in voluntarily. I was a phone call away from a call to Mama and access to a Greyhound bus ride home.

We collected hand-drawn maps of where we might go next, but we had to juggle practicalities and priorities when we fortuitously came across a good soul willing to take us a long distance in the general, but not precise, direction of choice. Also, if our ride planned to stay in a hotel for the night, we would ask to be let out somewhere along the road before it got too dark so we could figure out a field or hillside where we could set up our bed rolls for the night. Sometimes when it was raining, we stayed in the car for as long as possible, getting out at the last exit before our driver's hotel, stumbled up the freeway embankment, and wandered into the surrounds blindly, hoping we were not setting up in a dangerous patch and wouldn't be totally exposed come morning.

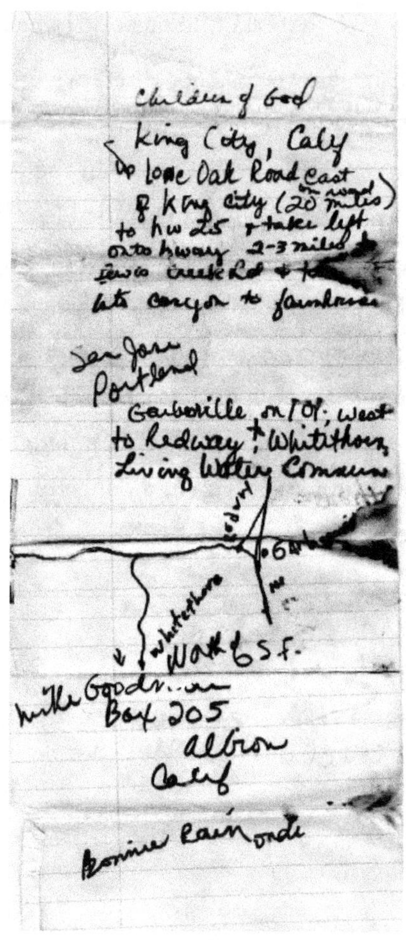

Photo 8: One of the hand-drawn maps we created and used while hitchhiking.

Surviving along the road, meeting new people, sharing views and stories, learning about how people talked and thought was truly enjoyable. People wanted to know why we were hitchhiking, what our goals were, and why a girl would be doing something they considered dangerous. Many wanted to share their views about politics and the war in Vietnam, whether we had (or wanted to buy) marijuana, and whether we were what they heard described as Jesus freaks. Sitting cramped in a car with heavy packs on our laps, for hours on end, was not that much fun, however, and was only made bearable by the thought of the alternative—standing out on the hot asphalt or in the cold rain for hours on end. We literally hitchhiked through Winslow, Arizona, ala The Eagles song "Take it Easy" ("standin' on the corner of Winslow, Arizona") during a spell when somehow we'd gotten off the main interstate highway. I recall exhausting, hot hours trying to look funny, adorable, earnest, and clean for the very few cars that drove by before finally getting a ride. But the thing I disliked the most was not being able to bathe or wash our clothes regularly. Every other week or so we would stop in a town and seek out a laundromat to wash everything we could and wash up in the bathroom. When we stayed at communes or people's houses, we were usually able to snag a shower, but we were reluctant to ask to wash our clothes. Often when we got in a car, I felt sorry for the driver who now had four smelly young adults crowded in their vehicle; I hoped for the back of a pickup truck on those occasions.

Along the way, we learned about people flocking to Calvary Chapel in Los Angeles, one of the early, highly successful "charismatic," evangelical mega churches. We eventually made our way there, but it was so popular and crowded that we never made it into the actual chapel but instead interacted with believers in a huge tent set up outside. Everyone seemed happy, but their focus was on prosperity and material goods (very "southern California," I later realized); it was not the kind of self-sacrificing, simple community that we were seeking. Also, we were reluctant to get sucked into another glossy church hierarchy that focused on fundraising more than fund dispersion; it seemed like a "hip" version of what we had recently rejected. Over the next few weeks, we experienced a variety of these types of evangelical, charismatic churches that were becoming popular where people would sing and pray and start "speaking in tongues," basically babbling word-like sounds that meant nothing, which is supposed to be what happened when the Holy Spirit came down upon the believers of Jesus, according to the New Testament of the Bible. Despite my intense belief in Jesus, I never felt an inkling of "tongues" bubbling up to my brain or lips. I felt guilty that I was not able to speak in tongues, and even more guilty for being cynical, but the analytical part of my brain told me I was most likely observing a form of group hysteria.

From Los Angeles, we hitchhiked north to visit a college friend of Charlie's whose family lived in Laguna Beach. Up to this point, we had no problem getting rides, sometimes the four of us crowding into VW bugs or other rattle trap cars, whose drivers often stopped along the road to harvest produce from ripening fields, then invited us to stay overnight and share a meal. But when we got to Laguna Beach, we entered the southern California of rising property values, individual wealth, and status. Though we had no concept of Laguna Beach vis-á-vis its chic reputation, we clearly stood out from the manicured people and their lawns. No one seemed happy to see the likes of us walking through their gated communities, and when we knocked on the door of his friend's parents' house, the welcome was icy.

"Hi! I hope this is the Smith residence?" Charlie asked as he beamed his most charming smile at Mr. Smith who had opened the door warily early on a Saturday morning.

"And you are . . .?" Mr. Smith asked. "Oh, a friend of Beth's I assume," he added after a moment.

"Yes, sir! I'm Charlie, and Beth and I were good friends back at Abilene Christian College and often worshipped together. My friends and I are hitchhiking up the California coast, and she asked me to look her up when I came this way," he said, gesturing back to Brad, Jeff, and I who were trying to look like promising young college students instead of the smudged and grubby hitchhikers that we were.

"Well, we just took her back up to Pepperdine University after a break at home. I'll let her know that you dropped by, Charlie. Stay safe out there," he said and started to close the door.

"Would it be possible for us to use your bathrooms, Mr. Smith?" I said before he could dismiss us completely. "We slept outside last night, and it would be wonderful if we could clean up a bit before we get back on the road," I implored, desperate to use the toilet and to brush my teeth. Reluctantly he opened the door, calling out to his wife that they had visitors while allowing us entrance to a beautiful home. We each took a turn in the bathroom, while the others made small talk with the parents and soon said goodbye and got back on Highway 1 headed north to Pepperdine to try to find Beth.

CHAPTER 6

CHILDREN OF GOD?

Fall 1973, On the Road, California

Charlie and Beth had been friends, with the potential of becoming something more, during her last term at Abilene Christian College before transferring to Pepperdine. They had talked via letter and maybe by telephone about the possibility of her travelling with us, and she had suggested they connect if he got to the West Coast. I remember a gorgeous college campus and trying not to think about the fact that she was moving on with her education while I had dropped out of college with less than one year left. The three of us made ourselves scarce by exploring the campus and environs, while she and Charlie talked. While she was glad to see him, she was not inclined to quit school and join us. Charlie was disappointed. Later I came to understand that Charlie was hoping to have a companion of his own, to offset the discomfort of constantly seeing me with Jeff. His romantic feelings for me went unspoken for years.

We headed north along California's Highway 1—stunningly beautiful but slow going—and then made our way over to Highway 101 with more traffic and thus more rides. We were accumulating names of promising sounding Christian communes that we wanted to visit, many of which were outside of small towns and/or in the countryside. We stayed at some for just a day or two and at others for longer periods, and a recognizable pattern emerged. Most nights featured a prayer meeting where the leaders focused on whatever belief or practice that they believed made them special in God's eyes, be it a way of speaking, type of dress, or food constraint. We hoped to find a group that looked past all these outward details and emphasized the big picture of God's mercy and Jesus's admonition to love one another and "judge not lest you be judged."

We stayed for nearly a week in one commune I recall, tucked away down a long rutted dirt road in the central valley. The days were warm in the sun and cool in the shade, and nights were brisk. The guys joined the other young men in the back of a pickup truck that took them to a local vineyard where they staked grape vines all day. I went with another group to an orchard down the road and picked apples. It was hard work, and we gained an appreciation for what it takes to bring quality produce to market. I also found out how delicious fresh-from-the-tree apples tasted. We were driven back to the farmhouse in the evening, had a simple supper with the other fifteen to twenty-five people staying there, and bunked on the floor in the house. Fresh-baked bread and eggs from the commune's chickens graced most meals. Most of the other commune members were our age or a bit older. Both men and women had long hair, while the men sported beards and the women wore all manner of clothing from free-flowing skirts to jeans or bib overalls. They were friendly to us but naturally cliquish having been there longer. Toward the end of the week, the group's leader, whom they revered, showed up.

"Hello, I'm Christopher," he said and shook our hands. "I had to go up the valley to check on some of our brothers and sisters working on projects there. I'm so glad you're still here because I wanted to meet you. Welcome!" He had a scraggly beard and salt-and-pepper greying hair pulled back in a ponytail. His handshake was warm, and he made eye contact with each of us before going into the kitchen and clapping others on the back or giving hugs. The energy of the place perked up significantly in his presence, and smiles replaced frowns from a hard week at work. We broke bread together, and then he commenced to preach his take on the important quirks of Christianity as he and his flock practiced it. He prayed that we would stay with them and become a permanent member of their group. He then disappeared back to his quarters. He was a nice enough guy, charismatic, like most of the leaders we met, but not compelling enough to make us want to live among them for long. We appreciated that everyone was respectful of our right to choose whether we stayed or not. We left the next day, disappointed that once again we had not found our people.

We traveled for another week or two before we closed in on the Children of God commune that was said to be near King City, California. We had finally gotten a detailed hand-drawn map for exactly how to get there and got a ride that put us along a two-lane country road, the final stretch. But night was drawing near, and there was very little traffic. It was late October or early November, and a cold front had moved through earlier. The rain had passed, but it was still cloudy and getting colder. On either side of the road, for as far as we could see, sat row upon row of freshly turned black dirt. This was not some mom-and-pop farm; we were in the middle of agribusiness—huge corporate farms owned by the likes of Del Monte or Hunt's, labored over by Mexican and other immigrant farm workers. We were just south of Salinas, California, and John Steinbeck's characters came to mind: the tired workers in "Of Mice and Men" and the families finally making it from Oklahoma in the "Grapes of Wrath."

Unfortunately, there were no nearby stores, no more cars travelling on the small road, and thus no food and no water. There were posted

"Keep Out, Private Property" signs but no fences to enforce the signs, so we trudged across the knee-high rows of dirt and prepared to bed down out of sight, a hundred yards or so off the road. That's when we saw small onions scattered all around. I assumed they were seed onions being planted. As I organized my bedroll next to Jeff's, I called over to Charlie.

"Charlie, what are you doing?" I asked, though I could see with my own eyes what he was doing.

"Eating onions!" he said. "I'm starving! Aren't you?"

"Sure, but not for those!" I said. "Who knows what kind of chemicals they use on them, Charlie, not to mention they haven't been washed. Ever heard of cow manure being used for fertilizer? Disgusting! Brad, is there any peanut butter left in that jar?"

"No, but there's still two pieces of bread. Here," he said and handed each of us half a piece of bread.

The light was fading fast. Resigned to a cold, hungry night sleeping rough, we placed our ground cloths between the rows, and Jeff and I put our Coleman sleeping bags as close together as possible before hunkering down and hoping to sleep.

I woke around 3:00 or 4:00 a.m. colder than I had ever been in my life. My teeth were chattering and my body shivering so hard I could hardly function. I realized my clothes were wet in multiple spots, though there was no sign of rain; in fact, it was a crystal clear moonless, starry night. Heavy dew had soaked through the cotton sleeping bag before turning to a scrim of frost along the outer lining. I was trying to figure out what to do about the cold when I heard an alarming rumble of large machinery getting closer by the second, followed by bright headlights shining our way. I sat up with a jerk just as a behemoth sized tractor crested the nearby hill and thankfully turned, going steadily in the opposite direction. I realized there were several other huge farm machines lumbering along nearby fields, though none appeared to be coming directly toward us now. I was not sure what to do about the machines other than jump up and wave my arms at them to stop if they got closer, but knew I had to do something about the dangerous cold.

"Hey, Jeff, wake up!" I said and shook him hard. His shirt was wet, too, but he didn't seem to be shivering like I was.

"What's wrong?" he said.

"The dew soaked through my bag, my clothes are wet, and I am so cold, I can't stop shivering. I can't get warm, Jeff. I need to get warm!" I said and got out of my wet sleeping bag. The part of the bag that had been next to the ground cloth was dry, so I sat on that and pulled dry clothes out of my backpack to exchange for my wet ones. I could hardly get my fingers to work, I was shaking so hard. Jeff got out of his bag, too, and tried to help me, but then he started shivering as well. Meanwhile, the farm machines were rumbling in the near distance.

"Hey, what's going on?" Brad said, his nose barely peeking out of his mummy bag.

"Our sleeping bags are soaked through, and now we are freezing cold. How are you?" I said. Brad had the most expensive bag of all of ours, with down filling, and he seemed to be warm enough. "I'm OK," he said, "but what's that sound?"

"Huge farm machines," I said.

"No, not that. Charlie, are you alright?" Brad said.

Now I could also hear it—Charlie was vomiting the next row over.

"Charlie, did you just throw up?" I said.

"Yeah, I'm sick."

"Are you wet and cold?" I said.

"I'm not wet, but I have fever and I'm sick," he said and rolled back into his bag.

I stomped around to try and get warm, and then Jeff and I tried zipping our sleeping bags together to have just the dry parts to cover us, but the fit was not good, and when one spot warmed up, the other side was more exposed than ever and freezing.

One of the longest nights of my life finally came to an end with sunrise, and we were grateful to start packing up our bags. Charlie was quite ill by then, feverish with bouts of vomiting and diarrhea. We had no food or water. We needed to get to the road and try to make it to the Children of God commune that day.

We believed our prayers were answered when we saw an old pickup truck come along the nearest farm road and saw a Latino family peering out to figure out who we were and what we were doing. We were disappointed when they turned onto the main road going toward town, the opposite direction of where we were headed. However, about twenty minutes later, as we were carrying our packs out to the road, they came back and waved for us to come over to their truck.

"Aquí, esto es para ti, amigos," the man said, and the woman passed us a loaf of bread, a jar of peanut butter, and a jug of milk. We gushed with thanks and relief, and Brad, who kept our combined funds in his bag, started searching for some dollars to give them. But they waved away our money, accepted our thanks and drove away. One of their kids called out, in English, "Good luck!" We stopped, held hands, said a prayer of thanks, and asked for blessings on the family. We kept them in our thoughts and prayers for a long time. Charlie drank some of the milk, and the rest of us ate, drank, and continued packing up our gear.

We eventually got a ride from someone who knew exactly where the commune was and took us right to their doorstep. We had finally made it to the Children of God commune, our original destination.

The commune members welcomed us, gave us food and water, and let us get cleaned up before assigning us places to sleep. That day and the next morning, we were asked to work in the kitchen and do household chores until they could fit us into their schedule. We learned that they hired out on local farms and knew their neighbors well, even co-schooling their children together, while also making sure they had a sustainable way to feed and care for everyone living there. The commune had some land to farm as well, and they grew carrots that they bartered with a nearby dairy farmer in exchange for milk from his dairy cows.

"Guess what?" I said to Jeff the next evening. "I get to be on the milking crew!"

"Is that a good thing?" he asked. "You'll have to get up at the crack of dawn, you know."

"Really, you think so?" I said. "Well, anyway, I'm excited to do it. I've always wanted to milk cows, and it feels like we're really living off the land."

"I'll be going out with one of the work crews and I'm not sure what we're doing, but it'll be good," he said. "How's Charlie? Have you seen him today?"

"No. Why don't you go check on him, Jeff? It's better if you check in case he's not dressed or something." He found Charlie only slightly improved, still weak and having episodes of stomach cramps and fever.

The next morning, the group leader woke me before the sun rose, and we loaded up the truck with milk cannisters and drove to the farm across the way. I loved the smell of the barn and the cows, though I had not fully appreciated how intimidating it was to be so close to such a large animal. I was enthusiastic about the milking chore but not very good at it. First, I had to learn to position the bucket such that the cow did not step in it or kick it over midway through the job. Then I had to learn the rhythm of milking, which is harder than it looks. I had filled less than a half bucket of milk by the time the experienced members of the group had finished milking all their cows and then came and finished my cow in ten minutes. The milk was pale orange because of all the carrots they foraged on. It reminded me of the color of creamsicle ice cream bars from childhood.

It was several days before Charlie was well, and we never knew whether it was from the onions he ate in the field or something else. The commune leaders made him stay in his room until the fever was completely resolved. They were worried because one of the neighbor children had just gotten over scarlet fever.

The group included fifteen to thirty adults and another five to ten children. The adults came and went during the day and evening, many working on farms close by. The others focused on the commune's proselytizing mission, which they carried out in nearby towns and larger cities. They handed out Children of God literature and especially looked for down-and-out youth to bring in for recruitment. Evenings were spent with domestic chores, fellowship, prayers, and readings from the Bible and from the group's leader who had taken the name Moses David.

One evening we took our supper plates, filled with our allotted share of food, and walked outside where we ate together in the dimming sunlight. It was the first time we had been together, with some privacy, since we had arrived at what had been our main hitchhiking destination. Charlie's illness and our varied work schedules had kept us apart.

"Aaron's nice," I said. "Bossy, but nice about it I guess."

"Yeah, I think he's the leader when Moses David is not here," Brad said.

"They have a bunch of rules," Jeff said.

We all nodded our heads in agreement at that and kept our voices soft.

"Did you see all the handwritten notes in the outhouse?" I asked. "'Only use three sheets per visit and not one square more!' and 'Jesus is watching! Do you really need more paper?' Sheesh! Do you think they have a Candid Camera in there?" Watching the TV show *Candid Camera* was a standard feature in most of our homes back then.

"Don't worry," Charlie said. "I used more than all our allotments combined in the past week, and I don't care if Jesus or Candid Camera was watching!"

We chuckled about that, and then Jeff said, "I think I got three more kernels of corn than I was supposed to. I'll need to confess and pray about that tonight in group fellowship."

Then Brad wiped his hands on a paper towel and took a folded-up pamphlet out of his back jeans pocket.

"What do you think about this, Susie?" Brad said. "Have you seen it? One of the guys just got back from a recruiting trip in the city. This is one of the pamphlets they hand out. I assume they especially target guys with this one," Brad said.

I took the pamphlet and read it again, having read it and others lying about the house. This one was titled "Revolutionary Women." The front cover featured a pen and ink drawing of a young voluptuous woman, and the next five pages were a detailed manifesto, ascribed to Moses David, which laid out his teachings about sex among The Family (i.e., members of the Children of God), in short verses, such that they could be easily quoted, I assumed. The essence of his teachings was that sex was God given and thus good. Men and women both liked sex but sometimes women got tired of it after they had children, so the Old Testament system of bringing younger women into the family made sense, according to him, to keep the men happy and let older women focus on their children and not be bothered by men and their sexual appetites.

We had heard murmurings about this aspect of the Children of God—how they believed in a Christian version of "free love"—but Charlie had seen no hint of it when he visited their commune in Texas a year earlier. We had hoped it was a false rumor, perhaps propagated by mainstream religions trying to discredit their work. But the pamphlet I read gave credence to the buzz on the street. The US and Europe were in the middle of a sexual revolution, the "summer of love" was still reverberating from San Francisco's Haight-Ashbury to New York's Greenwich Village, and it was little wonder that a segment of the "Jesus freak" movement might follow suit. The trappings of religion, with some fun.

The pamphlet was clearly a misogynist's manifesto cloaked in pseudo-religious mysticism, though I would not have had the words to describe it as such back then. I just knew it did not jive with my sense of self-respect nor what I thought Jesus Christ had in mind in any of His teachings. We asked the local leader about the free love aspect of the movement and their lives, but he downplayed it.

NO. 250   GP   "REVOLUTIONARY WOMEN"   June 20, 1973   MO

© CHILDREN OF GOD TRUST 1973. All rights reserved throughout the world. Reproduction in any manner, in whole or part, in English or other languages, must be accompanied by full acknowledgement of this publisher, including full name and addresses, and must be reproduced in whole without alteration or editing in any manner. P.O. Box 31 W.C.D.O., London WC1A 1AA England or Box 119, Dallas, Tx. 75221 U.S.A.

1. Those net stockings accentuate every little curve of your leg and increase the viewer's sense of perspective so that the curves are more pronounced and more discernible. It makes your visual perspective more accute. It reveals more of the third dimension and accentuates the positive. It's more glamorous. Any type of black lace net or mesh makes a woman's body more provocative. It makes you feel like you're seeing a little more than you ought to be seeing, which is exciting and provocative. And then there's draping, of course:—the Greeks found that draping with a thin material always accentuates the beauty of a woman's body and gives her grace and more flowing lines, following every little curve. The idea of clothing is to accentuate the positive! Clothing is like a picture frame. It should be as simple and plain and natural as possible, so as not to detract from the beauty of the picture itself. But it needs to be there to enhance the picture and accentuate it and protect it, but it shouldn't be so ornate, heavy, frilly or grotesque that the frame draws attention to itself rather than to the picture. The frame should also not hide the picture but should rather reveal the picture and actually beautify it, merely lightly drape it, surround it and bring out its beauty and set it off and apart from the rest of its surroundings, as clothing should do for a

Photo 9: Front page of one of the Children of God pamphlets widely distributed, circa 1973.

"Father David just means don't get all hung up on sex," he said, "and if you and your partner want to love other people, while loving and worshiping God, it's cool. But no one is forced to have sex with someone else in The Family, you know, or with anyone they don't want to. It's nothing weird like that, man. It's no big deal, really, but it's what outsiders like to focus on. It's their problem; you know what I mean, man? It's their problem, not ours."

We didn't know it at the time, but Moses David was on his way to becoming one of the major religious cult leaders of the century, and it was later revealed that he lived the life he preached. He had at least two wives and is alleged to have had sex, or facilitated sexual liaisons, with his children and grandchildren over decades. We never met Moses David, only his lieutenants.

I liked the homey feeling of the commune's workflow and the rhythm of the place. The people were friendly and down to earth, and the prayers seemed sincere. The warmth and water and food were also welcome after our difficult night in the onion field, but their adoration of Moses David, his writings, and the sex-focused pamphlets were worrisome. It certainly did not seem a substantive message for a life of service to God or the principles of Christ. After working with the group for about two weeks, we knew we had to make a decision: throw our lot in with the Children of God, or move on.

We decided to move on and left the Children of God commune on good terms, with an invitation to return if we changed our minds. We traveled north toward other groups we had heard about. Jeff and Charlie were enthusiastic about visiting communes in Canada if nothing came along before then. But I was less and less inclined to go further north, being convinced that we had nearly died of hypothermia in the onion fields of central California; worse would await us in Canada as winter loomed.

"God protected us in the onion field, helping us make it through the night, sending the family to bring provisions the next day and then a ride to the Children of God commune," Jeff said, certainty in his eyes and the set of his jaw. "Susie, fleshly harms and cold weather wouldn't have stopped Jesus. We are just weak because we have not been tried enough; we've been too comfortable in our middle-class houses. We can't stop now," he said, looking concerned that I would even consider the idea of not going on.

"I agree with Jeff," Charlie said. "It's been easy up till now to say we are trusting in the Lord. But He is just now starting to test us, so we need to pray more and have faith that He is guiding us. It's good that we will have the chance to fast for a few days now; I felt like we were getting too settled and fat staying at the last place for nearly two weeks, eating three square meals a day."

I looked at Brad, who said nothing. He did not like contradicting Charlie, but I was pretty sure he also had his doubts.

"The way I see it," I said, "God gave us brains, intelligence, and common sense, and He expects us to use them. My logic tells me that we are now headed into the time of year and the geography where weather can kill an unprepared person, and we are not prepared for Canada. We have no coats, gloves, or hats; our sleeping bags are rated for 40 degrees, not −20 degrees; and we have no plan of where we are going or how we will get there."

"Try to have more faith, Susie. You know I wouldn't do anything I thought might put you in danger. And let's pray about it," Jeff said, ending the conversation.

Self-preservation is an instinct honed over the ages among all living things. I hated feeling guilty about my supposed lack of faith, but I knew what I was saying made sense. I also hated feeling dismissed. I did not stop making my case, but we kept hitchhiking north.

CHAPTER 7

THEY'RE ALL F***IN' CRAZY

Fall 1973, On the Road, California

We had heard about a group of Christians living together deep in the redwood forests of the Shasta mountains near Ukiah, California. It took us several rain-soaked days of travel and sleeping outdoors to get close to the commune. One of the rides we got was from a group of guys in pickup trucks who asked Jeff, Charlie, and Brad to help them transfer boxes and crates from one truck to another along a remote road high up in the mountains. They promised lodging and a meal in return for the labor and a ride back out to the interstate the next day. It was heavily misting as afternoon turned to evening, and I waited for hours in the cab of one of the pickup trucks with a small affectionate dog. As night fell, they finished their work and drove us to a ramshackle house where they provided supper and a dry place to sleep. Afterwards, our hosts kept disappearing to a back room, coming back more and more drunk, high, or both.

As I was shaking my sleeping bag out on the living room floor, Jeff came close and spoke softly.

"Hey, Susie, we got a bad feeling about this place and these guys. We don't think we should stay the night. We need to leave once they're asleep," Jeff said.

"What do you think is wrong?" I asked.

"We're not sure," he said, "but we think all that stuff we moved today was stolen stuff or drugs or something. We couldn't tell exactly what, but when Charlie asked what we were moving, just making conversation, mostly, they got touchy, told us to mind our own business. We get the feeling they might not trust us to keep it secret, or maybe they want to rough us up and scare us or rob us. It just doesn't feel right. Anyway, keep your stuff together, and don't get undressed for sleep. They've been smokin' pot and passing a bottle of liquor around all night. It looks like they're all going to pass out soon."

Eventually everything was quiet except for guys snoring from bedrooms around the house, and we gathered our things and slipped out of the house in the cold, wet darkness. We stumbled around for a bit until we found the road we had come up the mountain on and made our way to the highway. We slept along the roadside until morning and then got back on the road headed to our next destination.

We finally found the redwood forest group late one afternoon, picked up by one of their members on his way home as we were searching for the correct turn-off. We were wet, cold, and hungry. The commune occupied a main house and a group of smaller cabins that we were told had been built by an earlier group of "hippies." The members warmly welcomed us in and invited us to eat our fill and then worship with them. The remains of their evening meal were on the table: canned peas, a loaf of Wonder bread, and butter. I am not a picky eater, but the one food I detested at the time was canned peas. That changed when my hunger was sated by the bowl of peas, which could have been manna from heaven for all I cared, creamy and delicious. I looked over at Charlie who, apparently, was having a similar food conversion. We kept eating until we finished them all.

During the clean-up, I had a chance to speak with one of the young women while the guys chatted up other commune members.

"Hi, I'm Miriam," the girl said, handing me a dish to dry. "My old name was Nancy, but I've been re-christened in the Lord since being here."

"Hi, I'm Susie," I said. "The one over there sitting by the fire is Jeff, my husband, and the one with the dark beard is Charlie; we went to high school together and were church friends from San Antonio. Brad is a friend from college. How did you find this place?"

"I'd say the place found me," Miriam said. "I was strung out, living on the streets in Sacramento after my parents kicked me out of the house. I was pretty bad off when Mark found me and offered to help me get clean. I came here and was able to kick my habit. This is day fifty-four since the last time I used. Praise the Lord!"

"Praise God," I said. I saw her smile over at a young man who was showing Brad what looked like a violin or viola in a case. Brad was a violinist, and he looked happy to be with a fellow musician.

"That's Mark, over there with your friend. We've been together since the second week that I got here," she said. "And that's Matthew, standing up and getting ready to pray. He's our leader."

Matthew was friendly, confident, and charismatic, but he had a dark-eyed, dark-haired deputy standing close to him who was the opposite, and we could see that others did not include him in the social chit-chat. He seemed very focused on our movements and conversations as we talked with people around the room. He gave me the creeps, and I avoided coming within his orbit.

Matthew called everyone to his attention and began a mixture of prayer and preaching.

"God, our Father, we thank You that You have sent these four children of Christ so they may help us in the work You have especially chosen for us. Just as we were despairing, You prophesied that they would be coming today! And as we finished our meal and some were losing faith, You delivered them to our presence! We praise Your name for Your blessings," he proclaimed to many "amen" and "praise the Lord" rejoinders. Others added their words of thanks to the Lord for our arrival, and on it went for some time.

It was strange to be the center of so much attention and we did not share their certainty that we were ordained to be there as permanent residents, but we took it in stride for the time being. We were tired and appreciative to be fed and looking forward to a warm place to sleep. We could lay fresh eyes on the group the next morning and learn what we could.

"Brother Matthew," Charlie said, "I thank God for your hospitality and warm welcome. We are strangers, and yet you have welcomed us like brothers and sisters as Christ would have done." This was also greeted with amens and "Praise the Lord."

"We have been living among groups of Christians since arriving in California a couple of months ago," Charlie said, "and continue to learn and pray and seek our place. We are happy to work among you to earn our keep while we discern when the Lord—"

Brother Matthew's booming voice cut into Charlie's speech.

"You see, children," he said, "tomorrow is the very day that we will be traveling as a group to our regional council meeting in Eureka where you can be confirmed by our brethren and leaders as part of our community. This is just one way in which we *know* that the Lord God Almighty has sent you just in time so you can get this confirmation. So go now, rest, and be ready to join us in the morning. Brother Jedediah will take you to your cabins." He left, hugging a few people on his way to the back rooms.

We tried not to show our surprise at being ordered around and said goodnight to the people we had connected with during the evening.

"Don't worry; you guys will like it here," Miriam said, her arm around Mark's waist. "It takes a little getting used to, but like any family, when we listen to Brother Matthew and the other leaders, work hard, and follow the rules, we have harmony and some fun too. You'll like the people in Eureka, and we'll have a potluck supper and dancing later in the evening before we come home."

"Yeah, get some rest, and we'll see you in the morning," Mark said, and they walked on.

Jedediah came up to us and pointed to the back door through a utility room off the kitchen.

"Meet me back there after you get your shoes on and packs loaded up," he said, "and I'll take you to your cabins." We did not talk among ourselves, leaving that to the privacy of our quarters. Once we were ready, we walked toward the back door where we saw Jedediah in the shadows of the utility room, talking to someone. As we approached, the scary deputy turned to confront us, blocking our exit. He got up in Charlie's face and spoke with intensity.

"You heard what Brother Matthew said, right? 'Cause it don't look like you get it. Your place is here, with us! That's an honor. That's a gift; do you understand? Are you going to accept God's will?" The guy spoke with authority, but he was not very big. It was not clear if Jedediah was backing him or wishing he could disappear. Jeff was not amused. I knew that look, and I could see he was going to shove or punch the guy any minute now—until the knife appeared.

The scary guy had pulled a large hunting knife out from a leather sheath on his belt. He jabbed the point into a wooden shelf next to the door as he spat out his next words.

"It is God's will that you came to us tonight, and we will make sure you do this bidding."

He removed the knife and stabbed it back into the wood before going on.

"Be ready to travel at 7:00 a.m. tomorrow and leave your things in your cabin. We'll be home by nightfall."

He took the knife out and put it back in its sheath, turned, and walked back into the kitchen. I would think of him years later when I saw photos of Charles Manson.

Jedediah led us out the door and escorted us to a cabin a five-minute walk away. It was raining again, a soft, constant drizzle that made it difficult to keep track of our directions.

"Here's the outhouse you can use," our escort said halfway up the path, "and here's where you two will stay," he said, "the Red Fern cabin." He handed Jeff a flashlight as he opened the cabin door. "The cabins don't have power, just the main house, and only when the generator is on. That'll go off in half an hour. C'mon, you two; I'll take you to the Fern Canyon cabin."

Alarm bells went off. We did not want to be separated.

"We can all stay here in the one cabin," I said. "I'm sure there's plenty of room, and we're used to it! We've stayed in much closer quarters many times." Brad and Charlie nodded in agreement and tried crowding in with us, but Jedediah blocked their way.

"No! I'm supposed to take you guys to this other cabin," he said and then nodded to me and pointed to a chair in the one room structure. "There are extra blankets on the chair if you need them. The wood stoves in these cabins aren't set up right now since they've been empty, but once we're back from Eureka tomorrow and you're here permanent, we'll get it working and it'll be plenty warm in here." His coat fell open as he started to close the door and we saw that he too had a hunting knife strapped to his hip. Two armed brethren. Protecting? Policing? Enforcing?

"Come on, now. It's starting to rain hard. Let's get you guys settled," he said, his voice trailing off as he led them down the path. After a few seconds, we cracked open the door and watched the sway of his flashlight to get the general direction they were going. It was dark other than his retreating light, and we had no idea which way the main house was, not to mention the main highway. We had been in communes we didn't particularly like or relate to before this, but this was the first time we felt danger.

Jeff and I used our flashlight to check out the tiny house, which was solidly built of redwood, with a small window on one side and a glass ceiling, which I imagined was a glorious skylight during the day. It was clean and smelled of wood and cold and wet, but the floor was dry and there was no evidence of past water damage. The contents were spare and included a cold wood stove and chimney flue in the corner, a single wooden chair, and a small wobbly table.

"I hate that we're separated from Charlie and Brad," I said, stating the obvious. "Do you think you could find their cabin?"

"Yeah," Jeff said," let's give it another few minutes, then I'll go that direction and see if I can track them down. But we should probably leave the flashlight here shining out the window so I can find you again."

"Good idea," I said. "Let's get our pallet figured out, and I'm going to try to find some dry clothes in my backpack."

A few minutes later, we heard a soft knock on our door and looked at each other. We had put a chair under the doorknob in hopes of keeping out the scary deputy and anyone else wielding a knife and looking for trouble.

"It's us! Let us in!" we heard Brad say. Jeff moved the chair and opened the door; Brad and Charlie piled inside.

"We are *so* glad to see you guys!" I said, and Jeff closed the door, replacing the chair under the handle. We sat in a circle on the floor, someone leaning against the chair and others against the wall. Our paranoia was such that we spoke in whispers, imagining guards or spies outside.

"OK, what are y'all thinking?" Charlie asked. "Brad, tell them what that guy with the violin told you."

"Well, first, he says he likes it here," Brad says, "and the fellowship is good, and he feels peace and the Lord's presence here. But I think the main reason he likes it is because he's got a girlfriend here, and the leaders are cool with that. He says the people usually get along, but there's lots of rules and that guy with the knife—Adam, I guess?—is one of the enforcers." He stopped and took a swig of water from the canteen he brought with him.

"But he thinks the reason they've been praying for more people to join them is because last week three of their members walked off a job in the middle of the day and never came back. The timber company guy they all work for was upset, and Mark thinks maybe they are threatening to cancel their contract. I guess that would be bad because that's how they pay their bills. He thinks that's one of the things they'll be talking about at the meeting in Eureka."

We digested the information as the rain continued its steady drumming on the skylight above.

"Well, I'm not staying at a place that needs someone like the psycho with the knife to make people stay," Jeff said. We murmured our agreement before he went on. "Their head preacher guy is alright, but he didn't say anything special, and so far, the rules seem ridiculous. One of the people I talked to showed me their weekly menu, which was hand drawn with beautiful fancy writing that said something like "The Lord likes peas on Thursdays," so that's what they have, peas every Thursday. Who cares about that? Where does that come from?"

"I talked to Mark's girlfriend," I said, "the girl with long red hair, who likes it here, but mostly because it's better than sleeping on the streets and they have helped her get clean from drugs."

"Yeah," Charlie said, "it feels like coercion, not Christ-like fellowship. And I agree with Jeff; the knife guy seems like a psycho just waiting to blow. Tomorrow is the perfect chance since they're piling everybody in cars to go into Eureka. If we don't leave then, we might have to wait another month to walk off the job like those other guys."

"But they said we can't take our stuff tomorrow, and I do not want to abandon it here," I said.

"Forget that!" Charlie said. "In the morning just be polite and smile, eat as much breakfast as you can, and act like we're happy to be here. But no matter what, keep your pack with you. Make up some excuse to take it so we can leave from Eureka. As soon as we get there, though, come together. We'll have to play it by ear and see how we can get away."

He took Brad's hand on the right and mine on the left, and we all joined hands and bowed our heads.

"Father, please protect us now in this place," Charlie said. "Guide us on the path to find Your wisdom and Your calling. Give us the courage to do what is right, for You. In Jesus's name, amen." We hugged each other, and Brad and Charlie made their way back to their cabin while we replaced the chair under the door handle and tried to make our cabin secure.

Jeff and I took off our shoes and placed them carefully by the chair. We took off our jeans as we slipped into the sleeping bags and rolled them up with our jackets to use as pillows, as usual. We turned off the flashlight and turned to face each other, holding hands until we fell asleep.

I remember the sound of constant rain that night, sometimes soft, dripping from the trees around us, other times thundering down on our tiny cabin. It was cold, and in the morning our breath made clouds of fog around us; but we were dry, and warm enough in our sleeping bags. We had slept very little, but we were anxious to begin the day and make our escape.

In the morning, we ate breakfast and sat on our packed bags while waiting for everyone to get organized. We were reminded to leave our packs behind, and we smiled and said, "Sure thing," but in the confusion of everyone getting into various cars, vans, and trucks, we held on to them anyway, got into the vehicles, and acted like we had heard nothing to the contrary. The ride to town was forty-five to sixty minutes through spectacular redwood forest beauty, but none of us could appreciate it; we were so anxious. The part of the town where the group met was near downtown, but it seemed like mostly vacant buildings and fenced-in parking lots. The caravan parked in front of an empty storefront. Two or three other groups converged on the site, and the people called out greetings, hugged, and shared updates. It seemed they met once or twice monthly to worship and socialize. There were thirty to forty adults, mostly couples but some singles. Two of the burlier guys stayed back near the doors we entered. Inside there was a large room with folding chairs set up for the group, and after an initial greeting by a more senior man, the four of us were asked to sit in front of the panel of leaders who welcomed us as their newest members. We sat in folding chairs with our backpacks firmly lodged between our feet.

"Welcome, Susie, Charlie, Jeff, and Brad," the leader said. He was a mid-forties year-old man in a T-shirt and Birkenstock sandals, beaming at us from a small stage at the front of the room. "God has brought you to us, and for that we are ever thankful. *Praise God!*" he said, again to many "amens" and "hallelujahs."

"Do not take lightly that God has a grand purpose for you among our people," he began his sermon, "for like Moses in the wilderness . . ." and on he went for some time, piling on the verses, pressing for us to accept it as God's will that we were there. Finally, we were given a chance to speak, and Charlie stood up, smiling his most genuine, self-deprecating smile.

"You have all been gracious, and it is a blessing to have found you and broken bread with you and learned about your mission. We also believe that the Lord is leading us and that we will know when we find the place where the Lord wants us to be. For now, we are still searching," he said and looked at us. In unison, and without ceremony, we stood up, slung our packs over one shoulder, and walked out the back of the room and onto the street, ignoring calls for us to return. The burly guys in the back kept chewing gum and didn't seem to notice anything amiss until we were walking out the door. They looked from us to the leaders in the front in confusion but did nothing.

We settled our packs on our backs and walked as fast as we could to the end of the block, twisting around a couple of times to see if we were being followed. We did not see anyone coming, but we felt vulnerable and exposed. Even though we were in the city of Eureka, all we could see were abandoned warehouses. My heart was pounding; I was certain the crazy knife guy was climbing into one of the vans at that very moment and going to come alongside and pull one of us in as a hostage. We turned the corner and ahead of us saw a familiar green "FREEWAY ENTRANCE" sign. We made a beeline to the on-ramp, walked directly past the famil-iar "Pedestrians, Hitchhikers, Bicycles Prohibited" sign, and stuck out our thumbs.

CHAPTER 8

HITCHHIKING TO MADNESS

November 1973 to April 1974,
Seattle, Washington to Corpus Christi, Texas

We would probably have welcomed a police cruiser but were even more thankful when an older pearl white Volkswagen Beetle pulled over on the shoulder in front of us. We grabbed our packs and ran toward the car. I got there first as the driver was leaning over to say something out the passenger side window.

"Hey, it'll be a tight fit, but where are you headed?" she asked.

"Hi, that's fine. We'll be happy to squeeze in and go as far as you can take us," I said and waved on the others. Three of us squeezed into the back seat, packs on knees, and Brad got in front, being the tallest of our group.

"Where are you guys headed?" she asked. Brad was the front seat person, so he was in charge of making conversation. We were happy to be safe and felt our pulses slow down. The tense night and lack of sleep from the night before started taking effect.

"We're not quite sure," Brad said. "We've been visiting Christian communes here in California, hoping we'll find one we want to join. But so far, none have seemed the right fit for us. We just escaped from some scary dudes back there in Eureka who were demanding that we join their group. We want to put some miles between us and them, and then we'll decide what's next."

"I hope you have winter clothes," she said. "You've heard the storm warnings, right?"

"No, what does that mean?"

"We're getting our first snowfall of the season, and it's going to be a big one. They are predicting blizzard conditions, and the passes might be closed. If you are headed to Seattle or farther north, you should get there in the next twenty-four to forty-eight hours, or you'll have to wait until everything gets plowed and opens back up."

"OK, that's really helpful to know. Thanks," Brad said and then turned around to see if we had heard. Charlie and Jeff were starting to doze, but I had heard what she said and nodded. I spent the next few miles putting this latest news into my growing unease about continuing the trip north, and Brad got out the map and started studying it.

Half an hour later she spoke again.

"Well, the next exit is mine, so I'll pull over and let you guys out. Good luck to you, and God bless!" she said and put on her blinker. Brad checked that I had heard, and I started shaking Jeff and Charlie.

"Wake up, guys. We're getting out here," I said while she slowed to a stop on the shoulder of the road before her exit.

Once we got out of the car, somewhere between Eureka and Crescent City, California, I unfolded the ink-stained raggedy note where we had written down church and commune suggestions and maps along the way. I studied both sides. "There are no more maps or suggestions here," I said and handed it to Brad who studied it and then gave it to Charlie who barely looked at it before he passed it to Jeff.

"And also, did you hear what she said about the winter storm that's coming?" Brad asked Jeff and Charlie. Yawns and sleepy faces looked quizzical, which I took as a no.

"A blizzard is about to hit the region, and the mountain passes will probably be closed around here and northward," he said. "It's supposed to start snowing in the next twenty-four to forty-eight hours, so we need to get someplace warm." We still had plenty of daylight left in the day.

"So, what's the plan?" I asked.

"God will lead us," Jeff said, and Charlie nodded his head in agreement. I like to imagine that I looked heavenward with skepticism, but I do not think I did—still trying to be the dutiful and prayerful wife and Christian sister.

"But practically speaking," Brad said, to my relief, "if we want to make any progress before a blizzard buries us, we need to stop travelling this coastal road and get over to Interstate 5." He set down his pack and took out the roadmap we had entrusted him with and laid it out across his pack. We bent down to study it. "We'll stay here on 101 North to Crescent City and then take this Highway 199 that cuts over across the border into Oregon and to Grant's Pass where it connects with I-5."

We were lucky to make it to I-5 before the rain started and even more lucky to get a comfortable ride all the way to the Seattle metropolitan area. We were quiet as the hours passed during the long ride, lost in our own thoughts about recent events and the future. I was beset with doubts about what to do. Was my reluctance to keep going north without a goal or plan because I lacked faith in God? Or was I not having enough faith in my God-given common sense and intelligence to stand up for my opinion and good judgement? Was I overstating the dangers ahead, or were my companions being blind to the obvious peril?

"Hey, it looks like we'll be passing right by the airport," I said, noticing a highway mileage sign.

"Yep, that's 'Sea-Tac,' the international airport between Tacoma and Seattle," our driver said. "Is that where you want me to let you off? It would be dry at least."

We came to a quick consensus and asked him to let us off there. We organized our gear and thanked him for the long ride. He let us off at the front entrance and waved goodbye. The weather was deteriorating, as predicted, with constant cold hard rain. The airport would be a safe and dry place to spend the night and make our plans. The time for discussions about "what next" was over, and a decision had to be made. Jeff and Charlie were intent on "following the Lord" even if it meant going into Canada, trusting that the Lord would provide and lead us through a winter of travel, if only we would have faith. Brad and I had expressed our skepticism already, and we were all just rehashing our same positions by this time.

We walked into the large airport, found a section of empty chairs in a waiting area, and set down our packs. Back then there was relatively little airport security, and there were no visitor screening procedures. Anyone could approach and sit around the gate areas. It was a relief to be warm and dry and not in danger from religious whackos in the forest or cops harassing us for being on the freeway. Jeff and I watched all the packs for a few minutes and then left our stuff with Brad when he returned. Then it was our turn to go find bathrooms and water fountains, clean up, and get vending machine snacks. We all needed some alone time to think.

Almost as soon as Jeff went into a bathroom and I was on my own, I knew I had come to a decision. I made my own pit stop and cleaned up a bit, then found the nearest pay phone and placed a collect call to my mother.

"Mom, it's me. How are you? I miss you!"

"Oh sweetheart, it is *so good* to hear your voice. I've been worried sick. I thought you would have called a week or two ago. I was so hoping you would be home for Thanksgiving. Where are you? How are you, honey?"

"I'm OK, Mom. But, Mom, I can't do this anymore. I'm not sick or anything, but it's getting cold, and I miss you and I want to come home. We are at the Seattle airport trying to decide what to do next. We are not finding anything that seems right in all the communes and churches we've visited, but Jeff and Charlie want to keep going into Canada to search some more," I said and started to cry, relieved to speak the truth about my fears and guilt.

"Well, honey, where would you go? Do you have another place to visit?"

"No, that's just it, Mom. We don't have any more ideas. We would just be traveling till something comes up," I said.

"Oh, honey, that's crazy! You don't have to go with them, you know. You absolutely do not need to do that. You make your own decisions!" she said.

"But, Mom, I'm supposed to be a faithful wife and go where Jeff goes; that's what the Bible says. But I'm just not a very good follower, Mom, you know?" I said and laughed just a little.

"I know that's true, Susie. I keep praying that you wake up and act like the common sense, sassy girl I've known since you were a toddler. I can't believe you still think all this is a good idea. You could freeze to death up there, for real!" she said.

"I've spent the last year trying to be an obedient wife, and I feel guilty when I try to lead from behind and frustrated when I try to dumb myself down and follow. But, Mom, we almost *did* freeze to death a few weeks ago in an onion field in the middle of California! There was ice on our sleeping bags, and I woke up wet and colder than I have ever been in my life!" I said and shivered, some combination of emotion and memory of that long night. "Have you talked to Dad lately?" I asked.

"He called a few days ago, also worried about you. He wants you to come home. But he doesn't have too much time to worry about us I guess, with his new girlfriend and her daughter keeping him busy," she said with disgust.

"I haven't told Jeff yet, but I'm going to figure out a way to come home now, Mom. Do you think you could send me money or buy me a bus ticket or something?" I asked.

We shared more tears of gratitude at hearing each other's voices and made tentative plans for me to find a Western Union office where she could wire me money for a Greyhound bus ticket home. I hung up and was the happiest I had been in weeks. My decision felt solid and smart and right. Now I just had to break the news to my husband.

I found Jeff pacing back and forth along a corridor. He had changed into a dry, clean T-shirt, tucked into his blue jeans, washed his face, and combed his longish curly hair, and looked as neat as he could given the days since our last shower. He also looked intensely disturbed and worried. I went to him, hugged him, and asked him to sit with me.

"Hey," I said. I took his hand in mine. "I love you with all my heart, you know? But I can't do this anymore. It doesn't make sense to me. Maybe it means I don't have enough faith in God, and if so, I'm sorry for that. But I want to go home now. I don't want to keep traveling with no idea of what we are doing or where we are going. I'm tired of having dirty clothes and barely ever getting to bathe and not being able to go to the bathroom when I need to." I paused to look at Jeff, but he was sitting stock-still, staring straight ahead.

"It scared me when we nearly froze to death in California, and now we have a blizzard bearing down on us. We were just threatened with a knife and almost kidnapped by people who believe in eating peas on Thursdays or whatever their rules were. If I thought we were in danger because we were standing up to an atheist, communist regime or something, or fighting for our rights to study the Bible or something, that would be one thing. But none of this seems especially holy or enlightened. It seems like we are putting ourselves in harm's way without good cause." He looked at me then, like he might try to counter my arguments like he had been doing over the past few weeks, telling me to pray about it and have more faith. But before he could say anything, I took a deep breath and finished what I had to say.

"I can respect if you feel you need to keep going," I said. "But I called my mom a few minutes ago. She is sending money for me to buy a bus ticket to go home. I'll wait for you in San Antonio, and maybe if you find a place that you think works for you, I could join you later or something."

He looked away from me then and kept looking straight ahead, minutes ticking by as he sat there, stone-faced, quiet. I kept expecting him to say something, but he said nothing. Was he fuming, disappointed, angry? Did he hear what I said? Then, like a dam breaking, tears began rolling down his face, and he could not stop them, no matter how hard he tried to brush them away. He blinked and shook his head but refused to look at me or say anything. He didn't look angry as much as he looked lost.

"Jeff, honey, I'm sorry. I love you so much. How about if we both just head home, rest, and rethink things? I am not rejecting you or your ideas, and maybe this is just a failure of faith on my part," I said. I had imagined my decision to be the start of an intense discussion or a heated argument. I assumed he would invoke love, obedience, guilt, or prayer to try to get me to come with him, or that he might reluctantly agree to go home with me and I would naturally feel even more guilt over that. What I had not imagined was that he would fall apart. Because that's what he was doing.

The shaking began as a tremor and then encompassed his entire body. I put my arms around him to try to contain his grief. He was in misery, and it was my fault. I wanted to make it go away.

"Jeff, please talk to me. It'll be alright. We just need to get through this together . . ." But he pulled away from me, his face in his hands, and his tears became sobs and then the words started.

"No, no, no. God, no, God, no, not this, not this," he said. He kept repeating the same phrases, and it sounded like he was saying aloud a conversation he had been having on the inside. He started rocking back and forth in the plastic airport seat and then stood up. His hands covered his face, but he kept sobbing and repeating the words, and then he walked away, sobbing loudly. I had never seen him so distraught, so undone, ever. I was also crying hard and was at a loss for what to do.

My instinct was to give him time and space to get himself together, so I watched him walk down the long corridor and turn the corner. I assumed he went to the men's room or some other private place where he could wail and weep. But the more I thought about his reaction, unique in my experience with him, the more concerned I became about the degree of his inner turmoil. I decided to follow him from a distance, just to see where he was going, to keep tabs on him. I rounded the corner, but he was gone. I waited for five to ten minutes to see if he would come out of the closest bathroom.

"Sir, excuse me. I think my husband went into that bathroom and he was very upset. Did you see or hear him in there?" I asked a man coming out of the nearest men's room. I thought Jeff would be embarrassed that I was asking for him like this, but I was too worried to care.

"No, I didn't hear or see anything," he said and hurried off, not interested in getting involved in someone else's drama.

After a few minutes, I called into the restroom, and hearing no reply, I went in and checked all the stalls. I then proceeded to do the same thing with all the other bathrooms and scoured every sitting area, restaurant, corridor, nook, and cranny. He had vanished.

I was starting to panic. I found Charlie and Brad and told them what happened. They were concerned but assumed he would show up soon, acknowledging that what I told him would, of course, be upsetting. After thirty to forty-five minutes passed, we posted one person to stay with the packs, in case he returned, and the rest fanned out to look for him, agreeing to meet back at the designated spot every fifteen to thirty minutes. After an hour or two, we sat down together around our back packs to figure out what to do.

"Tell us again exactly what happened, Susie," Charlie said.

"I told him that I couldn't keep going north," I said, "that it didn't make sense to me, and I was going home. I called my mom, and she can send money for a bus ticket. I told him he should go on if he felt he needed to but that I was turning around. He completely broke down crying and sobbing and saying, 'No, God, no!' Then he walked off, and I haven't seen him since."

"So, you basically told him you were leaving him," Brad said.

"No, I said I couldn't keep going," I said.

"But it's the same thing," Charlie said. "These past few weeks he's been more and more convinced that the Lord's will is for us to keep traveling until He puts the answer in our path. He talks about it all the time now. It's important to me too, but something has shifted in Jeff. He seems to have taken it to a whole new level. Now you are forcing him to choose; you or God."

"Yeah, I think it's a big deal for him, Susie. He's staked everything on this," Brad said. "Have you checked outside on the tarmac, Susie? You don't think he might try running in front of a plane taking off or something, do you?"

I looked out the large plate glass windows of the airport. It was completely dark outside, and the rain was now mixed with fat wet snowflakes illuminated by the massive headlights of the jets taxiing onto the runways for takeoff while others were landing before the blizzard set in.

They were right. For me, this was a relatively straightforward decision about going north or going home. But for him, this may have been an existential crisis. I knew he had become more immersed than any of us in the idea of finding God's plan, whatever that was, but so much that we couldn't discuss it? In the span of ten minutes, is it possible that my statement might have driven him to the brink of suicide? How had I not seen this possibility? I was bewildered by what had happened and about what to do next. But we knew one thing for sure—we had to find Jeff.

CHAPTER 9

NEVER MET A NUDIST I DIDN'T LIKE

Late November 1973 - April 1974,
Seattle, Washington to Corpus Christi, Texas

If Jeff wanted to kill himself, there were plenty of opportunities. Getting crushed by one of the airplanes landing or taking off in the chaos of the impending storm was just one option. What about the interstate right outside the doors? He could jump off an overpass or run directly into traffic. Would he do that? Can someone go from being somewhat broody and religious to potentially suicidal in ten minutes?

We found a pair of security officers, told them what had happened, and asked if we could report a missing person. They said they would tell their fellow officers to look for anyone fitting his description, but we would have to call the local police to report a missing person. I found a pay phone and called the police, but they said no report could be made until the person had been missing for twenty-four hours. So, we waited, we searched, we paced, and with great fear, we looked out at the runway and the fields beyond, imagining him waiting for the right moment to run in front of an aircraft. Once it was light, we walked outside around the perimeter of the airport, everywhere we were allowed. As the daylight hours passed, we retraced our steps and looked again. We were exhausted and took turns lying down in waiting room corners or on the seats, uncomfortable, jerky dream-filled REM sleep after having had very little sleep since before the Ukiah/Eureka debacle.

Finally, we deemed it was close enough to the twenty-four-hour mark and called the local police again and made the missing person report. By then it was our second night in the airport, and the security officers suggested it was time that we left since they had recognized we were not waiting to board a plane. We described our situation and the recently filed missing person report, and they agreed we could stay another twenty-four hours. Deciding it was highly unlikely that Jeff was anywhere inside the airport building, we situated ourselves so we could watch the front entry to the airport during the rest of the second night and into the next morning. We were haggard with exhaustion and sadness and at our wits' end about what to do next when two police officers walked through the front doors of the airport escorting Jeff inside.

We leapt out of our chairs and ran to Jeff, ecstatic to see him, hugging him and thanking the officers. Jeff said nothing to us and was completely without expression or emotion. He did not look us in the eyes and seemed vacant. The phrase that comes to mind is, "The lights were on, but no one was home." Apparently, he had walked out the front door of the airport shortly after he and I spoke and wandered around and into the surrounding neighborhoods, eventually making it to some sort of shelter. At some point he either discarded, or was relieved of, his clothes and now had on some unfamiliar threads. The officers said he had no identification and would not speak or give them his name. We assumed they only knew to bring him to the airport because of our missing person report.

Jeff was completely mute. He let us lead him to sit down, but he did not initiate any action or respond to conversation. He did not act like he was mad at me, or at any of us, or that he even remembered our conversation. It was more like he did not remember, or did not want to remember, how to interact with humans. It was as though his essence had been spooked and was hiding somewhere deep. During my subsequent medical training, when I read descriptions of acute combat-related shellshock, it reminded me of what Jeff was like then, and when I read about acute psychotic reactions, it makes me think that he was in a near-catatonic state.

It was obvious to the rest of us that trying to engage him with discussions about what to do next were pointless, and it was clear to me that we needed to get him home. He needed to be somewhere familiar, and I needed support so we could watch him and make sure he would not endanger himself. In retrospect, I know that the event represented his first psychotic break with reality, what lay people call a "nervous breakdown."

I do not remember many details past my surge of relief at seeing Jeff walk through the doors of the airport followed by my grief and trepidation at seeing the drastic change in him. We were all exhausted, and I was determined to take Jeff and me home. Charlie wanted to go to a place in Wyoming, and Brad was ready for home in Indianapolis. I do not remember calling my mother, but surely, I did. Why in God's name did I not ask for her to wire us two bus tickets? I have no idea. Instead, Jeff and I walked over to the southbound lanes of the interstate, I-5, where I stuck out my thumb to get us a ride headed south. We were going home the same way we got there—hitchhiking.

We were picked up by a most interesting driver, different from most others we had ridden with, who were often closer to our age. He was probably approaching forty years old, driving a nice, comfortable, big newish car—let's call it an Oldsmobile or a Cadillac since it was before the days of SUVs. I got in the front seat and made sure Jeff, still completely mute, was tucked away in the backseat, while I served as our conversation point person.

"Where are you two headed?" he asked.

"Home, to San Antonio, Texas," I said.

"That's great," he said, "because I came from Vancouver, British Columbia, this morning and I'm headed all the way down to Los Angeles. I need to get there by Sunday night for an early morning business meeting on Monday. I was hoping for help with the driving."

"I'm happy to drive," I said, "but Jeff is . . . not feeling so well right now. It's probably best to just let him rest."

"I see you're wearing a wedding ring. The two of you are man and wife, eh?" he said.

"Yes, we're not just 'shackin' up together if that's what you mean," I said, and we both laughed. "We are what you might call 'Jesus people,' and we've been visiting Christian communes Are you a Christian?"

It was great having an easy adult conversation in a warm, dry car with someone totally normal.

"I'm a nudist," he said.

I couldn't help but do a double take, making sure I hadn't missed total body nakedness or hairy knees sticking out from a trench coat. But he appeared fully, even warmly, dressed. He laughed at my reaction but with good humor.

"It's OK; I'm clothed as per conventional society!" he said, and I turned scarlet.

"I'm probably closer to Buddhism as far as religion goes," he said. "I believe our focus on outward, material things gets in the way of honest human interactions. It's harder to act like a pompous jackass when you're completely nude. I find that it's humbling and frees the spirit. People get down to genuine conversation and emotion when clothes are not there to speak for you."

He went on to say how being completely nude with others was not particularly sexual, though this was hard for my twenty-year-old self to believe. He and I had far-ranging conversations, and I learned that he was a chinchilla rancher in Canada and was on his way to Los Angeles for business related to that. Sadly, there were no soft furry critters to cuddle up with on the long road, alive or tailored.

Jeff was silent in the back seat, which was better than wailing or gnashing of teeth, which I half expected early on. As we approached the Cascades in northern California, there were flashing yellow road signs warning of a major blizzard ahead, and we were required to pull over and put on snow chains. Our driver was annoyed. He routinely drove every-where with snow tires alone and was certain he could get through any snow the lower 48 States had to offer. But the highway patrol would not let us onto the road to approach the mountain pass until he had the chains on, so both Jeff and I got out and helped him. He grumbled as he passed one after another white-knuckled driver creeping along the road at fifteen miles per hour. I was nervous but also excited, having never seen so much snow or driven over a mountain in a blizzard.

Once we got past the mountain passes of California, we stopped at a roadside rest stop, locked all the doors, and tried to sleep for a few hours. I think our driver was annoyed that his assumed third driver had not stepped up to bat, but he could see that Jeff was incapacitated. I didn't give him the details for fear Jeff would hear and act out again and because I didn't want to spook our driver. When we stopped at gas stations our driver brought snacks to the car for us. He was kind, and I was sad to see him go when he left us off at the intersection of I-5 South and I-10 West near Los Angeles. I wish I had kept his name and contact information. It would have been a real treat to have kept up with him over the years.

We got lucky again when we were picked up by a long-haul eighteen-wheeler going to El Paso. Jeff and I took turns sleeping in his cab bed, getting snacks, and cleaning up at truck stops along the way. He was clean, quiet, and no-drama, just looking for conversation and distraction. Two rides to get us from Seattle to El Paso was phenomenal, and we were in San Antonio in record time. It was late November when I called Mom from the outskirts of town, and she drove out to pick us up. I was embarrassed at how filthy and stinking we were but happy to be home.

We stayed with Mom who was still living at our old home in south San Antonio, and she and I drifted back into familiar roles where the mother ruled the household and I, the daughter, felt I was never quite living up to her standards. I had run my own household before, and it was hard being back in that role. But we loved each other, and it was clear that she appreciated my company.

"I went out on a blind date last week," she said. "Dottie and Francine and their husbands took me to a dinner-dance place and brought along a guy they work with. He was no Romeo, but he sure liked me!"

"Wow! Did you dance? How was that?" I said.

"Oh, yeah, we danced, and he held my hand and kissed me goodnight and wants to go out again this weekend," she said. I liked that sparkle in her eyes! I knew she was lonely without Dad and accepted wholeheartedly the idea of her meeting new men, in principle, but the idea of my mom as an attractive and sexual person was new for me. I needed to get on board with that idea, and quickly, I realized.

Dad was living with his new wife, Marie, and her daughter, Wanda. We met for breakfast and then went over to his new house.

"Sorry for the mess, Susie," Dad said and gathered up the dirty dishes, chip packages, candy wrappers, dog toys, and magazines layering every surface of the front room.

"Marie, hey! We're home! I told you I was bringing Susie over, and you said you and Wanda were going to pick up this trash!" he said. A girl came into the room in a furry bathrobe putting a finger to her lips.

"Shhhh! Mom is still asleep, and she was pissed off when I tried to wake her up a few minutes ago. Hi, I'm Wanda! You must be Susie!" she said.

"Wanda," Dad said, "I told you not to use that language, even though I know your mama does. It sounds trashy coming out of your mouth. Did you eat breakfast?"

"No, Mom never went to the store, so we don't have any milk or cereal. She said I should just eat Fritos," Wanda said, looking around for the half-eaten bag of chips that Dad had just thrown away.

While Dad was not yet conceding his massive mistake in exchanging Mom for Marie, the frustration and embarrassment on his face were plain to see.

Jeff's parents, Malvis and Walter, were welcoming and glad we were home and hoped we would get jobs and settle down. We were welcome to stay there for short periods, but the younger three brothers were still in school and at home, so the house was crowded. At loose ends, still in a seeking mode, and without a comfortable parental home to stay in, we hatched the idea to go live with former members of our Bible study group, a sweet, earnest young couple, Margaret and Stan. Stan was active-duty Navy stationed in Corpus Christi, Texas. Margaret was working as an elementary school teacher's assistant, as I recall. She was a stunningly beautiful young woman, the oldest of thirteen children, and she and Stan warmly welcomed us into their home, loving the idea of continuing our earlier Bible studies and Christian fellowship and happy to have us share rent and expenses.

Margaret and Stan had a meagerly furnished but large apartment close to the naval base, and we set up our sleeping bags on mattresses and began functioning as a family, cooking meals, and eating together, studying the Bible, praying, and singing together. Meanwhile, Jeff got a construction job, working when the weather was not horrendous, and I got a job at a plasmapheresis center processing blood donations to extract plasma.

It seemed the rain had followed us from Seattle, and there were many days in Corpus Christi when Jeff's construction job was on hold, leaving him sitting at the apartment alone stewing about what he should be doing next to satisfy the call from God. He became more and more talkative, but the talk was strident and militant about "doing the Lord's work," though exactly what that meant was never clear to me. For Jeff it meant *not* living in a warm, dry place but somehow suffering, and seeking ways to declare one's love and praise for God. More and more, he directed contempt toward me because I liked being settled, cooking and eating meals with friends, sleeping, waking up, and doing it all again.

His contempt rankled me, so I started pushing back.

"Jeff, why did you speed up and take that parking spot?" I asked.

"Because it's close to the front door, and I got here before her," Jeff said.

"But if you are all about doing what Jesus would do," I said, "isn't that an un-Godly thing to do? Shouldn't we park way back there to allow others to take the close spots? Or back there when someone tried to cut you off on the freeway and you yelled at him, shouldn't you just turn the other cheek and be happy that the other person got in front of you?"

He gave no answer but just glared at me like I was an idiot who did not understand the depths of God's purpose. For me it seemed like the only way to live a life of love was to . . . live a life and be as kind as you can when the opportunities present themselves. But I was trying my hardest to be a good wife, and by God I did not want that awful meltdown that happened to Jeff at the Seattle airport to happen again, so I clamped down on my criticisms. Meanwhile, Charlie, who had been working ad hoc construction jobs in San Antonio after returning from his extended hitchhiking trip after we split up in Seattle, came to visit, staying with Margaret, Stan, Jeff, and me in Corpus Christi for a while.

While Charlie stayed with us, we had a great many interesting and sometimes confrontational discussions about all the events happening in the world at that time, including the fact that we were experiencing the first oil embargo after OPEC decided to punish the US for supporting and militarily supplying Israel in its six-day Yom Kippur War in October of 1973. The religious zealots of the world had predicted Armageddon and the beginning of the end because of the Yom Kippur event, but that did not happen. Meanwhile, we were listening to the current hits being made by bands like Pink Floyd, Queen, Santana, and Chicago and still loved the Moody Blues, Jimi Hendrix, and the Grateful Dead. Many our age were dropping acid, and most at least occasionally smoked pot. It was popular to wallow in one's existential crisis and read books such as *Be Here Now* by Baba Ram Dass, which my cousin Wally gave me, suggesting this was another possible route toward spirituality.

We were getting restless at Stan and Margaret's house, and by April 1974, it was clear that they were ready to get their privacy back. They were, after all, still newlyweds. Jeff and Charlie and I decided we were about ready for another road trip, this time not focused on finding Christian communes per se but just generally "living life in the Lord" and seeing what happened. Though not in a drug-seeking mode, we were less dewy eyed than several months earlier and open to exploring what was happening out there in the world among people our age. I was hoping a change in scenery would get Jeff's mind off the dark cycles he kept returning to. The weather was warm, but just in case, we used our recent earnings to buy proper down sleeping bags, good boots, and a few compact camping items we realized would make our time on the road more comfortable.

Photo 10: One of the few surviving photos of Jeff and I during the year of hitchhiking. I am holding one of his nieces.

The three of us left San Antonio, still as God oriented as before, but disillusioned with the idea of finding an existing church or Christian commune that would suit our beliefs. We were still seeking where and how best to grow spiritually and hoped we would know it when we saw it.

CHAPTER 10

SKINNY DIPPING WITH THE HIPPIES

April-August 1974,
On the Road, Texas to Michigan and back again

We allowed the trip to unfold, sometimes headed to a friend's place, other times without a specific destination.

I recently asked Charlie what he remembered about Jeff's mindset and mental health at this point.

"I thought Jeff was making great progress spiritually," Charlie told me. "It was really during the second trip that I became close to Jeff as a friend."

"But I was also very uncomfortable, Susie, with how my presence was interfering with your and Jeff's privacy and intimacy," Charlie said. "If

I had been in Jeff's shoes, it would have driven me crazy to have my wife close by but not be able to be sexually intimate whenever I wanted. Over the years I wondered if that might have triggered Jeff to fall apart."

"It seems far-fetched to think that less sex is what caused Jeff's ultimate mental collapse," I told Charlie.

"I don't know if women ever really understand how most men think about this, Susie," Charlie said. "For me, and I think for most men, sex is synonymous with love in a marriage or other romantic relationship. More sex signifies more love. Less sex is worrisome—it might mean less love."

"You might be right, Charlie," I said. "But in my view, Jeff's lack of interest in getting back to a traditional married life, and my willingness to stay with him, was more telling than how much sex we had while we were on the road. Besides, when we got to a good camping spot before dark and were able to set up separate camps, Jeff and I did have sex; or at least I think we did."

Our first stop on the second trip was to reconnect with our former Highland Hills Church of Christ youth group leaders, Bill and Jane. They had left the congregation after our disfellowshipment and accepted a job at a Church of Christ in Houston. I hoped their ministry would provide a good example for us. In fact, I wondered if maybe we could work with them in Houston, but Jeff did not see their path as one the Lord wanted him to take.

"Susie, I must live a life in the Lord," Jeff said, "and do His good work. Don't you see? It is not an option!" Jeff's near-constant refrain always left me antsy and unsettled. What did he even mean?

"OK, Jeff, I get that. Fine," I said. "But like what, if not a ministry like Bill and Jane's? Join the Peace Corps and help people in Africa? Work for free at the homeless shelter or food bank? What is the action plan?"

I had to agree that the lives that Bill and Jane were living were more scripted and constrained than we wanted our lives to be, and they didn't press us to stay, so after a few days it was clear that it was time to move on.

Leaving Houston, we travelled west, making our way to a place we heard about in northern New Mexico, Arroyo Hondo. The word was that Arroyo Hondo was a good place to find kindred spirits, truth seekers who were living peaceably along the river. We had very specific instructions for how to get there and notes about natural hot springs near the river where people met. We were to look for a bridge off the main highway, and eventually we found the place, hiked a mile or more down a dirt road, and set up camp among the boulders that lined the river.

We stayed there for one to two weeks, setting up two poncho tents and bringing flat river stones up to a fire pit we created. A tiny store at the main road sold flour and other essentials, which we bought, and I proceeded to make flour tortillas in a natural concavity in one of the huge boulders. We also rummaged coffee cans from the store, which we filled with river water and tried to cook pinto beans.

Until this point, we had been teetotalers, abiding by the constraints of the Church of Christ rules. But while camping by the Arroyo Hondo, this changed.

We stood at the checkout stand of the tiny store with our second round of purchases for the week when Charlie set down a six-pack of beer. Jeff and I looked at him, and he looked only slightly ruffled.

"What?" he said. "Jesus turned water into wine. We've already been disfellowshipped. I'm in the mood for some beer."

And that was that. Having decided that alcohol was probably not truly a sin, the door opened for considering other drugs as well. We knew absolutely nothing about drugs or alcohol but decided we were not opposed to learning more. In fact, Jeff and Charlie began to consider the idea of the judicious use of hallucinogens to communicate with God.

Arroyo Hondo was a local destination because of the natural hot springs that bubbled up along the river, providing a perfect excuse for skinny dipping, i.e., swimming or soaking while naked with friends, family, or strangers, usually in a hot tub or warm spring. This was firmly in the category of what "hippies" did, and though I couldn't think of a verse in the Bible that prohibited getting naked with others, surely it was covered under one of the Ten Commandments . . . Maybe the lusting part? All in one week—beer and getting naked with strangers—praise the Lord!

When we got to the river and made our way to the springs, it was a very natural and wonderful thing to get naked and get in the water. There is a certain etiquette that applies—no direct eye contact before submerging, no direct staring at the private parts, that sort of thing—and once you figured that out, it was all good.

We met some friendly, interesting people at Arroyo Hondo, foremost among them Gene, a bit older than us, probably mid-to-late twenties, who was empathetic to our quest for spiritual authenticity and to Jeff and Charlie's tentative interest in taking hallucinogenic drugs for spiritual purposes. Gene and his companions were happy to explain in detail all the drugs they had experienced and each one's pros and cons. Despite their apparent vast knowledge of drugs, Gene and his friends appeared mentally sharp, quick-witted, and matter of fact; none of them appeared addicted to any of the substances and we saw no hidden agendas, i.e., they were not selling drugs and did not offer us anything except tokes of marijuana. They took special care to describe what to look for if we were to buy and eat peyote buttons, considered a natural, organic way to tap into the spiritual world, but warned that it was tricky to ingest enough of the plant substance to get high without first getting extremely nauseated from the strychnine-like substances in the buttons. They also warned us that lysergic acid (LSD) was often cut with nasty substances, and we should be careful whom we bought from. The purest form came in tabs of "windowpane," clear lysergic acid that had been absorbed onto blotter paper that could then be held under the tongue to absorb the drug.

I was interested in learning the details but had no interest in taking the drugs myself. My closest high school friend had taken LSD a few times and reported both amazing and terrifying aspects of her trips, including flashbacks for a long time afterwards. I did not like the idea of being out of control and feared being addicted to any substance. I also was not keen on the idea of Jeff taking any hallucinogens, especially given what happened back at the Seattle airport and some of his increasingly unusual ideas. I did not want to draw an absolute line in the sand, but I argued against the notion when it came up.

"We are headed out tomorrow," Gene told us one afternoon. "I suggest you guys wait to try any hallucinogens until you are in a safe, secure place. In other words, not here, along the river. It would not be the best place to be if things got weird." We agreed. The Arroyo Hondo camp spot was fine, but there were local people who walked along the dirt road day and night above our encampment and fishermen who walked down the river in front of our spot, who may or may not have our best interests in mind.

"I wanted to invite you to make your way to my place in Kansas in the next few weeks, if you'd like," Gene said. "I'm headed there now. My parents recently died, and my brother and I have inherited our family farm. This was my last big adventure before settling down to run the business and try to keep it from going bankrupt. I could make sure you got unadulterated clean drugs if you wanted to experiment in a safe place. Or you could just rest, maybe work some, and not do any drugs at all. There's a good group of friends and family who will be there, happy to share stories, philosophy, and food." We shared hugs, maps, and well wishes and bade him farewell.

We left Arroyo Hondo, New Mexico, and travelled to a place near Taos, New Mexico, where supposedly the American author and spiritual teacher Baba Ram Dass had gotten inspiration for his book *Be Here Now*, which we had read. It was difficult to get there, and what we found was disappointing. However, on our way back down the mountain, we met a young hippie family trying to make a living as organic farmers while playing rock and roll at Taos and other local ski resorts in the winter. Charlie helped the guy fix their broken-down farm truck, for which they were immensely thankful, and we stayed with them a few days helping around the farm. After supper they routinely put their three-year-old to bed and proceeded to practice with their electric guitars at full blast in the next room, well past midnight. Charlie got his guitar out and jammed with them, while Jeff and I held pillows tightly over our ears. I wonder if the poor child was deaf by age thirty.

We travelled north to Colorado Springs and then Denver where we worked for a week or so with a local temp agency. I was assigned work at a local hospital cleaning and making beds, and Jeff and Charlie worked with a moving company. From there we went to Boulder, Colorado, and met college-age members of the Soka Gakkai religion who invited us to stay with them indefinitely as long as we helped with the house chores and went with them to prayer meetings several times a day where people sat lotus style chanting "Nam Myōhō Renge Kyō" while thinking of whatever they wanted to attain: world peace, God's love, or a Mercedes Benz.

We finally said goodbye to the mountains of New Mexico and Colorado and made our way to Kansas and Gene's farm, near Lawrence. Sure enough, there was a warm welcome from Gene, his brother, and friends who were living there. We helped some on the farm, drank milk fresh from the cows, bathed, washed clothes, and delighted in the warm fellowship of young people like us, trying to "do the right thing" while figuring out what that meant. Several of his friends were focused on their own spiritual journey, though not necessarily a Christian journey. Unlike Christian communes we had visited in the past, no one was trying to establish a new religion and there were no prayer meetings or capricious rules about what to eat or wear. They were just working, reading, listening, arguing, and living.

Jeff and I were not especially close during the time at Gene's farm. I tried to draw him out, but he was not interested in anything simple or mundane, and when he did confide in me, I could barely follow his logic, much less his passion for such otherworldly interests. For example, he became obsessed with the idea of astral travel whereby someone supposedly travels through time, existing for a while in another time and place, learning some vast lessons from beyond the here and now. One of the other guests at Gene's farm was familiar with the concept, and he and Jeff spoke for hours about the possibilities. There were hours and maybe an entire day when I didn't see Jeff. He was off somewhere on the farm, talking to Gene or his friends or walking along the roads or in the fields. I tried to gauge Jeff's interest in taking hallucinogens like we had discussed in Arroyo Hondo, but he never gave me a straight answer.

"I'm not sure if Jeff ever dropped acid," Charlie told me recently, "but he might have. He and Gene talked about it several times. I'm pretty sure Jeff smoked pot though. I sure did. Gene and his friends grew their own and gave us both a bunch of it. I had never smoked before but decided to try it. I didn't know what I was doing, so I smoked a lot over a short time. I know it's supposed to make you mellow, but it made me hyper. I was so wired; I don't think I slept for a week, and I swear, it messed with my sleep cycle for years after."

Though I never learned whether Jeff took LSD or other drugs at Gene's farm, I know he became more paranoid and saw hidden meaning in everyday things, not bothered by the fact that he was the only one to recognize their significance. I could always find a logical reason for such events and was quick to lay out the explanations in detail—until the crazy cow event.

"Jeff, are you mad at somebody? I can hear you arguing all the way in here," I said one morning. I got out of my bedroll on the floor and found him pacing in the hallway outside our room. He was agitated about something and talking to himself until I came into his view. He directed his comments to me as though I had been part of a previous discussion.

"He doesn't know what he's talking about," he said, "but it doesn't stop him from saying whatever he wants and laughing like it doesn't mean anything. But I know Satan is real, just as real as God. The Devil is hard at work, and he's letting me know he's watching me; I see it now all the time . . ."

"Hey, don't worry about that guy downstairs and whatever he's saying," I said. "Let me get dressed, and then we can walk up the hill and see if we can get to that pasture where we can look over the valley, OK? It's beautiful up there, and it's not too hot so early like this."

I grabbed a couple of bananas from the kitchen. We went out the back screen door, past the chicken coop, and then started on the path up the hill. I tried to keep the mood light and his focus on the here and now.

"It's alright if he doesn't see things exactly like you do, right?" I said. "Everyone can have their own opinions. But what I want to know is, how are you this morning? Did you sleep much last night? It seems like you were up late and then woke up early. Did you get some breakfast?" In answer to the last question, he pointed to the banana he had just finished and threw the peel in the field. We had reached the first level spot on our climb, and we stopped for a minute.

"OK, banana breath, come here and give me a kiss," I said. I wrapped him up in a hug, and we began to kiss before I felt him pull back and stiffen.

He was staring open-mouthed at something behind me. I turned around and felt myself adopt the exact same stance before I rubbed my eyes and tried to figure out what I was seeing. A cow stood thirty yards away from us, her eyes rolled back in her head as she tried to walk, staggered, and nearly collapsed. She flung her head and horns about and bellowed loudly in mental or physical anguish; we didn't know which. Her eyes focused somewhat, and she walked in a wide circle, round, and round, tossing her head now and then. Wide-eyed and shocked, I looked at Jeff. I had no logical explanation for what we had just witnessed and it made the hairs stand up on the back of my neck, but I quickly rejected the notion that it was anything supernatural. I now suspect that the cow was sick with bacteria called Listeria that causes a syndrome called "circling disease." But Jeff was certain that he knew what was going on: Satan was delivering a warning to him that bad things could happen to him too if he wasn't careful.

After a week or more at Gene's place, Charlie split off to visit other friends, and we hitchhiked to Indianapolis where we visited with our former co-traveler, Brad, who had abandoned physics and was following his true passion, music and violin. We had dinner together, and it was good to see him happier than he had ever been at Abilene Christian College or traveling around the country. We then headed north to Bloomfield Hills, Michigan, where our former apartment neighbors in San Antonio lived and worked.

Jane and her husband had lived upstairs from Jeff and I during the first year of our marriage. Jane was my married-lady mentor. She was a masters level teacher by profession, and while her husband served out his military service at Brooks Air Force Base, she enjoyed being a full-time mom to her adorable baby daughter, Heather. She had a radiant smile, was mature, funny, loved to cook (often calling her ma on the phone to get clarification on an authentic family Italian recipe), and happy to be my older married girlfriend and guide. She had given me the lasagna recipe years earlier and howled with laughter when I told her I had not boiled the noodles first. In the evenings, we sometimes grilled burgers or steaks together, though our husbands didn't have a lot in common. Her husband, whom we knew by his nickname, Snuffy, delivered withering commentary about the ineptitude of the US military, the imbeciles in the US Air Force, and the idiots who called themselves Texas politicians. He couldn't wait to go back to Michigan and start law school.

We had let Jane and Snuffy know approximately when we would be visiting and had also given our families their address to forward mail to us. When we got there, I imagine they were anxious to get us off the front porch of their very upscale neighborhood and into the shower/laundry room ASAP, but they were friendly and welcoming. They now had a toddler son, and Heather was not a baby anymore and, of course, did not remember me, but we quickly became reacquainted. We were happy to see that there was mail for us including a thousand-dollar income tax refund from the time we worked in Corpus Christi. We had settled into a convivial evening meal around the dining room table when the phone rang.

"It's your dad," Snuffy said. I went to the kitchen to take the call.

"Hi Dad! This is a surprise! Is everything OK?" I asked.

"Susie, oh thank God, I found you!" Dad said. "Your mother . . . Honey, your mama . . ."

"What? Dad, what? What's happened? Is she alright?" I said. I heard him blow his nose on the other end of the line and try again.

"Edith's been diagnosed with breast cancer, honey. She's been admitted to the hospital and is going for surgery tomorrow morning. She's been trying to contact you at all the addresses you left with her. She wanted you to be there," he said, his voice breaking again, "and she couldn't find you, so she asked me to keep trying."

"What? Oh Dad, no, no, please no!" I cried.

"She's having double mastectomies, and they are worried that it has spread," he continued. "Can you come home soon? I feel so helpless not being able to be there with her," he said.

I was shaken to my core, trembling, sobbing, beside myself with the need to be there at her side. Jeff came and stood next to me and got the gist of the conversation. My mother was facing a life-threatening emergency alone, and here I was thousands of miles away. What was I thinking? How could I have thought that being so far away from the people I loved the most was alright?

"Dad, I'm going to get there as soon as possible. I'll call you right back, as soon as I figure out our plan," I said and hung up the phone. I turned to Jeff, and we sobbed together until the urgency of the situation overcame our grief long enough for us to make a plan. I knew he felt as anxious to get home as I did. Jane and Snuffy were standing by, ready to help.

She already had her travel agent on the phone, and with our tax refund in hand, we were able to get on a flight very early the next morning. It was the first time either Jeff or I had ever flown on an airplane. I remember being surprised at the magnitude of power I felt as the plane gained momentum and lifted off, but there was no joy in this new adventure. I assume we had a layover, but I have no recollection of any of that, just an intense and visceral need to get to my mother's side.

Dad picked us up from the airport. He had visited her the night before, so he knew where to go. It was already past the time scheduled for surgery, but we headed toward her room anyway to check the status when we saw a gurney escorted off the main level elevator. I dropped my back-pack at Jeff's feet and ran down the hall. She looked over, saw me coming, and opened her arms for me.

"See, I told you she'd be here. This is my baby girl; this is my Susie," she said, words slurring and her eyes dreamy looking as she took me in her arms and let me cover her face with kisses.

"She's had her pre-meds," the escort said to me, smiling a little.

"Yeah, I got the happy juice already!" she said with a giggle. "You just wait over there in my room, and I'll be back before you know it. Now that I know you're here, it's all going to be just fine," and she started to drift off.

CHAPTER 11

LIFE GETS REAL

August to November 1974, San Antonio, Texas

Mom had no complications from the surgery, but it was a big ordeal. She had to get blood transfusions while in the hospital, and she was weak and tired for weeks afterwards. Every bit of breast tissue and lymph nodes were taken from one side and a less radical lumpectomy performed on the other side. The cancer had already spread to lymph nodes, so surgery was followed by radiation therapy and chemotherapy.

We talked for hours during her recovery. While driving back and forth to radiation treatments one day, she told me how she had found the cancer.

"Dr. Glickman discovered the breast lump about six months ago, maybe nine months," she said, "but you know, he's Aunt Louise's doctor, too, so he assumed that it was fibrocystic breast disease, like she has, and not cancer. He had the nurse show me how to do self-exams, made me feel the lump, and told me to come right in if there was any change at all."

"So, what happened? Did it turn to cancer without ever changing?" I asked. She was quiet for a minute, looking out the car window, and shook her head.

"I noticed it was changing," she said, "getting bigger, getting hard. But frankly, I didn't care. I knew I should call the doctor, but . . . I couldn't get up the energy. I can hardly get up the energy to eat these days. I've lost twenty-five pounds since Dad and I divorced, most of it since Jim and I got married."

"Mom, it sounds like you've been depressed," I said and reached over to take her hand.

"I hate to be ugly but being married to Jim is worse than being alone," she said. "It's not that he's mean to me, but he's not very smart, and he's not good at much of anything, so that makes him defensive and controlling and . . . Let's just say, he's not your dad; that's for sure.

"Thank God I have my job," she said. "My friends at Randolph Air Force Base are great. They think I'm smart, and funny, and know I work hard. I get together some with Louise, but she's busy, and the family get-to-gethers are not much fun for Jim. He's a big stick in the mud, and then he gets jealous and huffy when I try to do anything without him.

"Anyway, other than work, there's not much that I look forward to every day. When I went back for my six-month follow-up, which I was late in scheduling, Dr. Glickman examined me and I thought he was going to blow a gasket, he was so upset. 'How did you not see what was happening here, Edith?' he said. I was crying, and I think he was, too."

Back then there were no mammograms, no ultrasound-guided biopsies, and surgical biopsy was not a trivial endeavor. Plus, the doctor had a plausible explanation of fibrocystic breast disease, which indeed, runs in families. He obviously did not recognize her depression and did not guess that this mature, practical, and savvy woman would watch passively while the mass grew. I can imagine his horror at palpating the enlarged mass, its fixed and firm nature telling him without a doubt this was cancer, and then feeling the enlarged lymph nodes under her arm. I know he visualized all the lost time since their last visit during which the nasty cancer cells had time to double, double again, and double again, loosen from one another, travel through the blood stream, and seed every place they could reach.

Most of us learn to fear and worry about cancer when we hear that an acquaintance or public figure has succumbed to one of its myriad forms. Sometimes it comes closer: Hodgkin's lymphoma killed a junior high friend of mine. Now it had my mother in its crosshairs. At that moment, my hatred for cancer became personal. And my dislike for Mom's husband, Jim, was headed in the same direction.

Jeff and I stayed with Mom and Jim while she recuperated. Mom's illness made it abundantly clear that life was short, and it was time to get real and move on. I knew what I wanted to do next: get my college degree. I hoped Jeff was going to get back in a groove soon. Mom and I were a great team; I helped with dressing changes and then put soothing Keri lotion on her healing wounds, and she and I debriefed about our lives since we'd been apart. Despite having a dreadful diagnosis and having to deal with the consequences of surgery, she had snapped out of her depression and had a great attitude.

"Well, if some part of me had to be taken away," she said on more than one occasion, "I'd rather it be my breast instead of one of my arms or eyes or legs. I'm not having any more babies, so I don't much need my breasts anymore. And I'm not letting this damn cancer take me yet! I still have too much I want to do!" I was happy to see her acting as though she deserved to be listened to and that she deserved to be happy. She talked back to Jim when he acted jealous or controlling or derisive and let him know how she felt about anything and everything and spoke up for what she wanted and did not want to do. She reminded him that she had managed her life and her own finances just fine in the year after Dad left and before Jim cornered her into marriage.

It was mid-to-late August, but I was still able to reenroll in school and start the fall semester on time. Until classes started, I shared the cooking tasks with Jim, and later Mom, went to the store, and ran errands as needed and helped keep the house clean. Jim went to his civil service job by day; nights and weekends he puttered around, muttering negatively about everything, while I tried to ignore him. He had made my mother sad, somehow using her to make himself feel less inept, so I was not inclined to like him. But then his little dog, clearly resenting our intrusion into his space, nosed our bedroom door open one day when we were out, found the boxes of family photos Dad had recently brought to me, and systematically chewed, tore, and peed on the lot of them. When I came home and discovered the mess, Jim just smirked and declared that it was perfectly understandable for the dog to protect his territory that way. My vague contempt for Jim and his dog turned to disgust.

I called my friend Kathy one day, to catch up and find a time to get together.

"Hey, Kathy, guess who? We're back!" I said. I told her about Mom's cancer diagnosis and surgery and a summary of our hitchhiking adventures. "And I'm back in school, finishing out as a biology major and chemistry minor," I said. "I also plan to get a teaching degree. Jeff's looking for a job. What's up with you? You finished your med tech degree, right? Are you working?"

"Of course, I'm working, woman. How else would I pay the bills?" she said, and we laughed. It was good to hear my friend's voice.

"How are the boys? And are you still living in the little house out back from your mother-in-law?" I asked.

"Well, there's a lot of news on that front. The boys are fine, growing, and healthy. And they love having their dad back at home," she said and paused to let that soak in.

"Oh, so he's out of Huntsville," I said. "How's that going?"

I heard her sigh and then call to her mother-in-law in Spanish.

"I just asked her to watch the kids, and now let me close this bedroom door and get some privacy," she said. After a moment she came back on the line. "I'm pregnant," she said. "Again."

"Oh . . . OK, congratulations! I think?" I said.

"Yeah, well, not what I had planned, that's for sure. I knew his release date was coming up but expected to get a few weeks' warning. One night I heard a knock on my door, and there he was. Oh, Carol, he'd already been drinking before he got there, but he wasn't drunk, and I couldn't really deny him his first night out of prison . . . and now I'm pregnant. Due in May," she said. We talked for a bit longer before she had to go intervene in a ruckus with the kids but promised to get together once I had a break from school.

While Mom was gaining her voice and her will to live and I got organized for school, Jeff wandered around the house aimlessly, stewing about life, God, and what he was supposed to do next. We agreed on one thing, though—it was wonderful to have a comfortable bed and privacy. So, it is a wonder that I, a twenty-one-year-old biology major, was so shocked when my mother looked at me in the kitchen one morning and let me know that I was pregnant.

I was making coffee when Mom came in and sat in the chair at the breakfast bar.

"Honey, when was your last period?" she asked after watching me for a few minutes.

"That is so weird you would ask that, Mom," I said, "because I was just thinking it should have started last week or the week before. I'm usually so regular! Of course, now that I'm off the pill my periods are not as regular as they used to be . . ." The wheels started turning in my head as I heard my own words trail off.

Mom just shook her head in wonder and said, "You know you're probably pregnant, right?"

I remember staring at her like I had never heard of such a thing. Sometime in the past six months I had stopped my birth control pills; Jeff and I had decided it was hypocritical to be "trusting in the Lord" for so many other things while not trusting pregnancy (or not) to Him as well.

"Mom, what do you see that makes you think this might be true? How can you tell?" I asked, starting to let the possibility seep into my consciousness.

"Well, you've never really had much in the way of boobs before, and now you clearly have a bustline, and your face is just the slightest bit fuller. Also, I notice you've come home and taken a nap every afternoon this week; that's unusual for you. And see how the veins in your hands are more prominent . . ." she trailed off, eyebrows lifted and head cocked.

I was a roil of emotions when I went back to tell Jeff Mom's observations. He just grunted, disbelieving. I called her obstetrics-gynecology doctor's office and arranged to go in that day and get a pregnancy test that, of course, was positive. I went from being shocked to not being able to keep the grin off my face within a few hours. Mom knew how hard parenting could be and had real trepidation about Jeff's state of mind, but she loved the idea of being a grandmother. She and I quickly transitioned into problem-solving and planning mode. I had just restarted school, hoping to finish college by the following May, but that timing should work out fine. A person can still go to school while pregnant, no problem—check. Jeff had not yet secured a job, but he was a young, healthy man; surely, he could get something, maybe get hired back at Southwest Bell Telephone company, right? Check. Surely this news would sweep all the grandiose save-the-world obsession out of his brain and help him focus—we had a baby coming! We could live with Mom and Jim for a while more, but we needed to find some other place to live so Mom could figure out what was next with Jim and we could start our lives with a new baby!

Jeff was just as shocked as I was but did not get to the happy and grinning stage. He acted like I had somehow tricked him into the situation. I talked, cajoled, reasoned, and reckoned for hours until he finally agreed that, yes, it must be God's will for me to be pregnant, because . . . I was. Following this line of reasoning, it seemed clear to me that it must also be God's will that Jeff find paid work so we could move on with our lives. Eventually he seemed to agree, but every few days he would lose his resolve and fall back to a more vague but grandiose plan for saving the world.

"Jeff, why are you scowling and looking so unhappy? How did the job search go today? Anything look promising?" I would ask in the upcoming weeks.

"I didn't look for jobs today, Susie. I spent the day thinking about what I should do and praying for an answer. And I got an answer, Susie. Yes, I did!" he would say, looking at me, both defiant and accusatory. "All of this, getting pregnant and going back in school, it's all a way to suck me back into the comfortably numb world of men, instead of following the Lord. God is testing me," he would say.

While I hated hearing it, most of his words were consistent with the same dreary cycle he had been in for months now. But then he added in a new element that saddened and alarmed me:

"Satan is using you, Susie, to get to me. I know that now. You are trying to tempt me to stay here with you, using your womanly wiles, just like Eve did with Adam," he said, "and I know I have to resist you!" I tried to talk reason to Jeff but found that nothing I said made a difference. After a few days, he seemed to get back on track and start looking for a job and say the right words about being a supportive husband and father-to-be. A few days of hope would be dashed when his next cycle of anguish started. I wanted the Jeff I had married back in my life. I wanted to think about the baby growing in my belly, and preparing for childbirth, and making a nest for our child.

I called my friend Kathy back just three weeks later with my own surprise.

"Hey, Kathy, it's Carol," I said.

"Hey, did you already find time to work me in your schedule? You must have a light load in school!" she said.

"No, I'm calling because I have news. I'm pregnant, too," I said.

"Holy moly, woman. Are you happy?" she said.

"Yes! And no," I said. "Sometimes when Jeff sleeps in and I get to take the car and drive myself to school, I sit there between classes and just cry. Jeff's in a cycle where he's angry all the time and thinks I got pregnant to interfere with his ability to 'serve the Lord,' whatever that means for him, that day.

"It occurred to me the other day," I said, "how definitive it is to be pregnant! There's no opportunity to reset the timer or negotiate for a different start date," I said.

Kathy laughed. "Yeah, I hear you on that one! The timing never seems right. But there are options, Carol. Adoption? And abortion is legal now, of course," Kathy said.

"I know there are options," I said, "but I've always planned to have children, and I believe it is God's will that I am now pregnant. We've been living a prayerful life, and we agreed to trust in the Lord when I stopped taking 'the pill,' so I must believe that my being pregnant is His will and He will protect and care for me and the baby, for all of us. I just wish Jeff had a job and we were not dealing with his emotional roller coaster!"

"I got lucky," she said. "When I registered at the Robert B. Green hospital—that's the clinic for us poor people, you know!—they set me up with a certified nurse midwife named Hoffmaster. She's wonderful. If Jeff doesn't get a job and insurance soon, check her out." I filed that information away but already had an appointment with an obstetrician one of my aunts had recommended.

Like my friends, I was intent on everything "natural": childbirth, breastfeeding, and baby foods. The question among my peers was not if you wanted to have a natural childbirth, but whether you wanted to give birth at home versus at a hospital. Lamaze classes for natural childbirth had become popular, and the La Leche League was spreading the gospel of the superiority of breastmilk over infant formula from a bottle. Unfortunately, the doctor could not have been less to my liking and not at all in sync with my interests. He was highly experienced but old school and condescending. After examining me, he told me my due date would be May 12, 1975. He also said to forget about natural childbirth because my pelvis was flatter than normal and I should prepare for a forceps delivery if not a Cesarean section. I asked tons of questions, but he essentially told me to not worry my pretty little head about so many complex things but just lie back and enjoy the "twilight sleep" he would give me when the time came and leave the rest to him. It turns out he was right about my anatomy, but I never went back to see him again.

Jeff and I lived with Mom and Jim for about two months. I don't know where we got the money—maybe Jeff got a temporary job?—but at some point, Jeff told me he had rented a garage apartment for us to live in. I was happy that he had taken the initiative but had to stifle a gag when I walked into the place that first evening. When we turned on the kitchen lights, there commenced a fluttering and rasping of large flying cockroaches finding their hiding places. The kitchen sink and toilets were stained and rank. Dead insects and a musty smell filled every corner. We had a roof over our heads, running water, and electricity, but I would have traded a night on the road at the mercy of the elements over this hellhole any day.

We moved a mattress into a corner of the single bedroom, and I scrubbed the kitchen and bathroom, saying little to Jeff while I worked. I didn't know what to say. What was he thinking to bring us here? I went to school, and we had a few meals there before Jeff's mood swung back to agitation and paranoia. I woke up one morning to find him packing his belongings into the car. He was determined to "follow the Lord" and became angry when I tried to persuade him not to leave. But he drove off anyway.

I despaired that there was no end to these cycles. I prayed and cried, in sadness, frustration, and mounting anger. I was better than this. I felt certain Jeff would return, but in the meantime, I needed some help. I went to the owners in the main house out front and called my dad from their home phone.

"Dad, we moved out of Mom and Jim's place," I said, "but now Jeff has decided he has to go somewhere and do something related to 'following the Lord' and left me here with nothing to eat but a loaf of white bread and no way to get groceries. Can you bring me a few things?"

When he found the house and walked inside, Dad's face registered disgust, disappointment, and anger.

"Susie, my God," Dad said, "what the hell? This is Jeff's idea of a place for you to live? And then he abandons you? I'm ready to knock some sense into that boy. Honey, you can't stay here. Is that where you sleep?" he said and pointed to the mattress in the corner. "With mice and rats all over the place . . ."

"I haven't seen any mice, Dad," I said, mortified.

"I can smell them," he said, "and look there in the corners; those are all rodent droppings. Oh, no, you can't stay here. This is . . . Pack your bags. We're getting you out of here."

I was ashamed for him to see me there and doubly ashamed to admit that Jeff had driven off that morning, supposedly gone for good, to "follow the Lord," leaving me with no car, food, or money.

Dad was desperate for me to come home with him, but I was convinced Jeff would not be gone for long and wanted to be there when he returned. It was time for a reckoning.

We ate the burgers he brought while sitting in his car, and reluctantly Dad left me there with a few grocery items but not before going to the owners and demanding that they get an exterminator to the property to deal with the cockroaches and rodents. He vowed to return the next day after work and take me to his home or Mom's.

I spent the rest of the afternoon studying in the kitchen that I had scrubbed as clean as I could get it. Jeff returned before dark and found the screen door locked.

"Susie, are you in there? It's me. I'm home. Let me in. Please, let me in," Jeff said.

I went to the door and looked out at him, a book in one hand, the other on my hip.

"What? Oh, you're back now? What happened? The Lord didn't give you an address?"

"Susie, I realized I can't leave you and the baby. It's just not right. I'm sorry. I'm so confused," he said and started crying.

"Jeff," I said, "I'm not going to sit around and be the consolation prize for when you don't get a clear message from God. My father had to come over and bring me food, and you know what? He was so disgusted he refused to eat inside the house. We ate hamburgers in his car."

Jeff looked like he wanted to crawl into a hole.

"Dad's coming back for me tomorrow. I'm not living here with you. It's disgusting and humiliating that you brought us to this place and then abandoned me. I figured you'd be back, so I stayed to tell you I'm done with all this. You want to leave, then leave. But I'm done being the yo-yo."

"Susie, you're right to be angry with me, but I've got a grip on myself now. I know I need to stop thinking so much. I promise I'll be a good husband. I'll get a job and make it right."

It was music to my ears, and I agreed to give him another chance, though I was skeptical.

We moved out of the vermin-infested hovel and in with Jeff's parents. My mother-in-law, Malvis, was a very practical, down-to-earth, kind-hearted woman. She and my mother were very different from each other, but I loved them both. Malvis loved big gardens and eating fresh vegetables, digging in the dirt and saving scraps for the dogs and cats she rescued. She believed the Bible, went to church regularly, and rarely cursed but also knew that nobody was perfect. She was able to laugh at her own and other people's weaknesses and foibles. She walked the walk of Christian ideals as best as she could. She had been working at the San Antonio Mental Hospital for several years as an attendant and often came home with funny and sad stories about the "crazies" there. When we moved in with them, she witnessed Jeff's outbursts and mood swings and was concerned that he looked a lot like the patients she worked with.

Jeff's family had switched to a different Church of Christ congregation after our disfellowshipment.

"A bunch of us agreed that Ted was on some kind of power trip," Malvis recounted one Sunday after they returned from church, "so we started visiting other congregations. We found one we like, and you'd recognize quite a few old Highland Hills church friends who moved like we did. In fact, today the Crossens asked about y'all and offered up an empty trailer home they bought for one of their kids. The utilities are paid, and they said you could live there a few months, rent free, till Jeff gets a job and you guys can get settled."

The manufactured, or "trailer" home, was on a half-acre of land in north San Antonio. It was a new neighborhood that had fifty to hundred side-by-side half-acre fenced-in lots; many lots were still empty, and others had their own mobile home in place. It was a strange neighborhood, but the home was modern, clean, and comfortable with a fully equipped kitchen and clean carpets. We were grateful and moved in with only a mattress on the floor of one bedroom, a sofa that someone gave us, a clock radio, and a small black and white television. Compared to the place we had just left, it seemed like heaven.

CHAPTER 12

MURDEROUS INTENT, PART 2

December 1974, San Antonio, Texas

I was fully engaged in school now working on finishing a degree in biology with a minor in chemistry and a certificate to teach secondary school. As a senior in college, I had a full load including several independent study classes and projects. Jeff took me to school most mornings and picked me up in the afternoon. When not in labs or classes, I camped out in the school's library, which I remember as always being cold, winter or summer. Every afternoon at around lunchtime, I used the library pay phone to call my mom at work, and we talked freely for most of the hour on most days.

"Guess who I spent the afternoon with?" Mom said one day.

"Other than Jim?" I said.

"A man, a very sexy man who seems to like me very much," she said.

"OK, well, that's not Jim. Mom, what are you talking about? Are you having an affair with someone?" I asked, happy and scandalized. She laughed at my reaction.

"Your dad bought a small used RV and moved it to a little park near the Air Force base where he goes on the weekends to get away from Marie. He asked me over for an early supper, and I said yes, and well . . . it was very nice," she said.

"You're having a secret affair with *Dad*?" I whooped. "I love it!"

"He grilled steaks," she said, "and baked potatoes and asked me to make a salad, and it felt so good to have conversation and just be ourselves. He said that getting divorced from me was the biggest mistake he ever made. And he said marrying Marie was the second biggest mistake."

"Well, amen to both of those things," I said.

"He hasn't left her yet because he feels sorry for her daughter, who Marie either ignores or makes fun of and barely cares for. It's sad, but he's not going to change Marie. And I don't think he's got it in him to sacrifice his life to be a dad to Wanda. But he's got to figure that out. In the meantime, we're just going to take a little time now and then to be together and get to know each other again." I could hear the sparkle back in her voice. It was intoxicating for her to be the "other woman" for a while.

Of course, I also talked to her about Jeff, but other than being supportive, she was at a loss for what I could do to get him to snap out his obsessive cycles. One person I would have turned to for solace and advice was our friend and former hitchhiking partner, Charlie, but that relationship had gone cold, though I did not understand why until years later.

I knew that he was back in school and trying to complete a degree in engineering, and I had heard he was back together with a previous girlfriend. He knew I was pregnant, and his mother told me he was using his woodworking skills to start working on a baby cradle for us in his dad's shop. But the cradle never materialized. All I knew was that he did not call to check in on us and seemed aloof, and Jeff seemed more agitated, not less, if I mentioned trying to connect with our old friend.

Recent conversations with Charlie helped me piece together the basis of our estrangement. He told me about an incident that occurred when he was home from college in 1974, probably for Christmas break, and staying at his parents' house, which would correspond to the time when Jeff's connection to reality was becoming tenuous, though Charlie did not know this.

"I had given Jeff the book called *Time is the Simplest Thing*," Charlie told me recently, "a science fiction book about telepathic travel, which I thought he might like given our talks about astral travel while we were at Gene's house in Kansas. I had forgotten all about it, but one day I was working out back in my dad's woodworking shop when I saw Jeff walking up the sidewalk, unannounced. I stopped what I was doing to go and greet him, but before I could even say hello, he got right up in my face and confronted me saying, 'Why did you give me that book?' It took me a minute to figure out what he was talking about, but then I said, 'I just thought you'd like it.' 'Don't give me that!' he said and demanded again, '*Why* did you give me *that book*? There *is a reason*. Why did you give it to me? What are you trying to do to me?'

"I was baffled about why he was so mad," Charlie said, "and especially why he was bringing it up at that time. 'No reason, Jeff,' I said, or something like that. But that wasn't a good enough answer, so he got even closer, purposely stepping on my toes and grinding his boot down hard saying, 'What are you, chicken? I can take you! Let's go!'

"Well, of course I didn't want to fight Jeff," Charlie continued, "but this was typical for him when he got mad or defensive about something. But in my gut, I was certain that the real reason he was there, and why he wanted to fight me, was that he was jealous over you. As much as I had tried to clamp it down, I believe he could always sense my strong feelings for you, Susie."

"Aha. Let's talk about that," I said.

"I was in love with you since I first started seeing you at church when we were in junior high or earlier, Susie," Charlie said. "I never thought you would give me the time of day, so I just tried to content myself by being your friend and pretending that was alright. When in high school, we practiced guitar together at Danna's house and sang for the soldiers at Brooke Army Burn Center, I was mostly doing those things just so I could be with you."

"Charlie," I said, "why didn't you ever say anything? I felt there was something between us, too, but you always seemed so churchy and righteous, and anytime there was an opportunity for something other than friendship to blossom, it seemed like you would turn distant and back off, and that made me think I was imagining the whole thing."

"I was stupid about girls and women for a long, long time, Susie," Charlie said. "I had no idea how I should feel or what you might feel. I was too insecure to say anything. But I can tell you that I was crushed when you announced that you were marrying Jeff after high school graduation. I realized I had lost all chance of trying to be with you. But I also hoped that maybe your marriage would put an end to my being in love with you.

"I thought I had succeeded," he said, "until we started studying the Bible together, went through the disfellowshipment together, and then started hitchhiking. All my feelings were still there, and I battled against being jealous and angry at Jeff most of the time. It was a trial to be so close to you but not physically with you."

"And Jeff knew," he said. "I felt certain that, somehow, he knew."

"What makes you think that?" I asked, though I knew he was saying something I had felt as well but had never articulated.

"He probably saw me when you and I were talking or doing something together while we were on the road and could tell how connected I felt with you. Maybe it's just a guy thing, but I know he felt it. I think that's why he was always trying to outdo me. If we were moving boxes on a job, he would try to move them faster or carry more of them than I did. If we lifted something heavy, he would make sure to lift something heavier than I did," Charlie went on. "So, his belligerent behavior that day at my parents' house seemed in keeping with all that, and I was tired of it. So, I told him to get out and not come back. We didn't fight, but I decided he was being a jerk and I just didn't want to be involved with him anymore," Charlie continued. "And now I feel bad about that, Susie, because I had no idea about the hard times you were going through or that he was mentally insane. I cut you guys off, thinking it was better for me and better for the two of you if I was out of your lives."

Theoretically, Jeff was out looking for work each day that December, although this was not going well, either because he never made it to the interview appointments or he did not really make any appointments. Each day was a crap shoot when he picked me up at school, whether he would be clear-eyed and rational, or shifty-eyed, quiet, and paranoid. My mantra became: if things are going badly, just try to wait it out, but if things are going well, get prepared because they are going to turn nasty. There were occasional good days, and early on I would let myself believe that maybe the nightmare was over. But these became less and less frequent. I didn't have the vocabulary or psychiatric background to know that he was having auditory hallucinations, but I did know something was going on in his head that no one else could see or hear.

I had always been a high performing student, making As and Bs in college except for a C in organic chemistry that I crammed into one summer after my freshman year of college. My teachers expected, and got, full and enthusiastic attention and effort from me. That fall semester, however, there was so much chaos in my life that I had a difficult time keeping up. We had moved from Mom and Jim's house to the reeking hovel, then to Jeff's parents' house, and now to the trailer house in the boondocks, all in the span of about ten weeks. I was still in my first trimester of pregnancy, and though I rarely vomited, I was exhausted to the point of nauseousness most afternoons. Evenings were filled with rants and arguments with Jeff, and though I studied during the days at the library, I was increasingly distracted by Jeff's erratic behavior, his recriminations, and judgments.

The days blurred together during November and into December. Jeff's cycles of lucidity and insanity came faster and faster, with fewer interludes of sanity. He got sneaky and started to get mean. I remember fearing the worst when he would pick me up from school and be sugar-sweet to me. By the time we got home to the trailer, he would bait me into saying things that sounded like *I wanted* to have a calm, normal life and *not follow God*, that *I believed* that going to school to get a degree in biology and a teaching certificate *was important*, that having a clean home, food on the table, and warmth in winter *mattered*, that being pregnant with our first child was *a good thing*. All of which I did believe, but it sounded like heresy when he said it, when the words were hurled at me like they were sinful and self-serving. The trailer house on half-acre of land in a quiet neighborhood started feeling less and less like an oasis and more and more like a prison.

Eventually the paranoia and badgering and intimidation became physical. He would not let me leave the trailer without him and hid the keys to the car. When I tried to walk out the door in the middle of an argument, he would block my exit, grab me painfully by the arms, and force me back into the trailer. His sleep schedule became chaotic and his agitation level high. I knew things could not go on like this for much longer.

Jeff picked me up from school one afternoon later than we had agreed on, and I was ravenously hungry and exhausted to my core, a state typical of first trimester pregnancy. I could tell Jeff was in a mood. During the ride home he was ranting about Satan, getting more and more agitated, and inferring yet again that I was purposely trapping him with my pregnancy.

"Jeff, you know what?" I said as we approached the house. "If you think God needs you to leave and go do something else, then go. Just go. I am not going to beg you to stay. Drive me to my mother's house, and then just keep going. If you don't want to be a dad or stay with me, then I don't want you here. Just go!"

He ignored me and kept up the barrage as we walked into the trailer house, and despite my exhaustion, I considered escaping his tirade by walking out the door up the road or even driving off in the car.

As though reading my mind, he jingled the set of keys before locking the dead bolt on the only door out of the trailer and stuffing the keys deep in his jeans pocket. He'd never done anything like that before, and it gave me pause. I was angry, but I also sensed that something was new. This was different; he was different. He was someone different. I tried not to think about the locked door and to stay calm.

I started making supper because, despite my exhaustion and apparent captivity, I was shaky from hunger. I hoped that by doing something normal and routine he might calm down, but I also knew that anything domestic and "normal" might also trigger derision and cynicism. But I had to eat, so I began peeling potatoes. Jeff came into the dining area off the kitchen and then turned on the clock radio, playing random music at maximum volume.

He stood at the kitchen counter and made fake small talk in a sing-song falsetto voice.

"Making a nice supper, are you, Susie?" he said. "Little Miss Susie homemaker you are, aren't you? Nice day at school? Got to hang out with your school friends, did you? Got any boyfriends there, Susie? Do you?" I tried to ignore him, but he grabbed the half-peeled half-cut potato out of my hand and yanked me to him, holding me forcibly against his chest. He jammed the half-cut potato against my cheekbone and just stood there smiling at me.

I couldn't budge against his hold, but I tried to make light of it and get him to loosen his grip.

"Jeff, you're being silly. What are you doing with that potato I'm about to cook for our dinner?" I said and tried to wriggle away.

But his false smile became a sneer, and his grip on me was intentionally painful. I dropped the potato peeler on the counter as he dragged me out of the kitchen.

"You like to dance, right, Susie? You say I never dance with you, so here we are. *Dance*, Jezebel!" he said. He pulled me around the room, twisting and circling until I was stumbling and dizzy, all the while crushing the cut potato against my face.

"OK, Jeff, no more dancing," I said. "You're hurting me now, and I'm tired and hungry. In fact, I think I might be sick. Let me go now! This can't be good for the baby," I said. He ignored me. He kept up a verbal tirade about how I was holding him back from his mission for God, my lack of faith, my lack of sincerity, my insistence on what was practical, what I thought was sane.

When he finally let me go, I went into the bathroom and tried to lock the door, but he followed me there and stood in the doorway while I retched and then peed. I walked past him, angry, crying, and at my wits' end. I gave up on dinner and curled up on our mattress on the floor of the bedroom, facing the wall and hugging a pillow to my face. I did not think I could bear the exhaustion I felt. After a few minutes he knelt beside me.

"Turn around," he said.

"No! I'm exhausted and I need to sleep. Leave me alone," I said.

He grabbed me then and forced me onto my back. I saw that he had taken off his jeans and T-shirt. He was naked and ready for sex.

"Jeff, leave me alone. What are you doing? Just leave me alone!" I said, but he started pulling down my pants, pushing me back onto the mattress when I tried to stop him. "Please! Stop! You're hurting me!" I said. "I don't want to have sex with you now. You're being mean, and you're not acting like yourself. Leave me alone!"

"I'm going to treat you like the daughter of Satan you are, like you deserve!" he growled.

I yelled, bucked, thrashed, and swiped at his face until he bound my hands together again over my head with one hand while forcing my legs apart. He was too strong for me, pure and simple. I begged him to stop, then gave up, and asked him to be gentle, to remember our baby was inside of me.

He was not making love to me, and it was not consensual sex. It was an assault. He was angry and controlling and wanted to hurt me. He was trying to punish me on behalf of his gods or his demons. I was under his control and powerless. I begged him to stop, worried that he would hurt the baby because he was thrusting so hard, but he did not stop. I realized I didn't even know who this man was. He was nothing like the Jeff I had married five years ago. I finally went still and let him keep going until he finished.

All I could think was, "My husband just raped me. I will never forget this. I hate him. I hate him. I hate him."

Sleep overtook Jeff soon after he raped me. I lay curled on my side until I was sure he was in deep. Then, I went out to the front room and cried until I puked. Empty and numb, beyond exhaustion, I stared out the window for a long time.

I had no doubt, now, that Jeff was insane, psychotic, crazy—I didn't know the right term, but something was badly wrong in his head. The person I dealt with that night was not the same as the boy I grew up with or the man I married. He needed help before he or I got hurt or killed. But it occurred to me that perhaps there was another way: maybe I could join him? Why was I holding on to this thing called sanity? Why did I insist on an objective reality, prudent and predictable behavior? He had inexorably crept to and now gone over the edge; why not join him? How hard could it be? To have and to hold, in sickness and in health, for better or worse, right?

But, of course, I could not decide to be deranged, just like he could not decide to snap out of his delusional spiral. Though it seemed like he was choosing insanity, because the trappings of religious zealotry were familiar,

I knew it was an illness that was consuming him. He was not choosing mental illness any more than a child would choose polio or a young mother would choose acute leukemia. So, I was sane, and he was not.

The next morning, I thought I was going to be safe once we made it to Jeff's parents' house. I also thought Jeff would get help a couple of days later when he agreed to see the emergency room psychiatrist. But I was wrong on both counts. I found myself once again in his control, locked in a bedroom staring at the glinting edge of honed steel that Jeff had prepared earlier in the day so he could cut what he believed was the child of Satan from my belly.

Jeff held the knife in his right hand and gripped both my hands in his left, ready to perform some crude butchery in God's name. I had no more illusions. He had raped me a few days ago; he might kill me today. My bloodstream was flooded with adrenaline, and I easily broke free of his one-handed grip. I flung myself against the locked door and began screaming and pounding.

"*Help in here! He's got a knife!*" I said to the door, hoping someone in the house would hear me.

"Susie, just calm down! You know this is *God's will!*" he said.

"*Jeffrey, get away from me! Put the knife away! What are you doing?*" I said while screaming and kicking and twisting away from him. "*I know you don't want to hurt me or our baby, Jeff! Please, think what you're doing!*"

I kept my back to him and shielded my belly while screaming for help. He tried to peel me away from the door, but I stayed strong. Soon I heard voices and chairs scraped against the floor in the dining room outside the door.

"Jeff, what are you doing? Stop and open this door, *now!*" Walter said. "Susie, what's going on?"

"He's got a knife and says he's going to cut the baby out of me!" I screamed.

"Malvis, get the screwdriver in the top drawer! I might have to get this door handle off. Call the police, and get Kyle in here!" Walter said, calling for Jeff's younger brother.

"It's none of your business, Dad! Just leave us alone! This is between me and Susie and the Lord," Jeff said.

I strained to stay as far away from the knife as I could. At least with Jeff distracted, he was not actively trying to slice me.

"Move, Dad!" Jeff's brother Kyle said when he got there and then kicked and slammed his sixteen-year-old body against the hollow door, which finally gave way. The youngest brother came running, and together they tackled Jeff and held him on the ground with the knife pinned against the floor. Malvis got me out of the room. Jeff struggled to get free, but it was three against one.

"The cops are coming, Jeff. You better calm down!" Kyle said.

The police arrived, two cars and four men, lights and sirens ablaze, and without hesitation they were through the front door and back in the bedroom. They asked if anyone was injured, and when we said no, they muscled Jeff into handcuffs and marched him out the door. Walter and Kyle went with Jeff and the police outside, while another officer stayed with Malvis, Dwight, and me. I was dry-eyed, but I could not stop shaking. We gave the officer details and background about Jeff's recent mental state, and after thirty minutes or so, the other police brought Jeff back into the living room with us.

"My partner says he did not cut you or hurt you. Is that correct, ma'am?" said the lead policeman who had been outside with Jeff, acknowledging me for the first time. The shakes were calming down, and reality was setting in, what he had done or nearly done, planned to do.

"He didn't cut me, sir. My father- and brother-in-law broke in the door just in time—"

"Well, that's good, Mrs. Green. I'm mighty glad to see that. We've had a good talk with Jeff outside, and I think he's gotten his mind straight now. He says he didn't really mean you any harm and has been under a lot of pressure lately. We've explained how serious this is, and he says he's sorry and he is going to get some help," the policeman said and then turned to Jeff.

"Is that right, Jeff? Are you going to apologize to your wife and family like we talked about out there?" the policeman said.

"Yes, sir, I apologize," Jeff said.

"Say it to them, son; they're the ones you upset," he said.

Jeff turned to face me, but his head hung low and his eyes stayed on the ground.

"I'm sorry, Susie. I really am," Jeff said, and his voice broke. "I keep going back and forth between knowing you're the one I love and this notion about what I need to do for the Lord. It made sense in my mind that somehow you did it on purpose, getting pregnant and all. Anyway, I just got confused. I'm sorry, and I'm going back to see that psychiatrist from yesterday and see if he can help me." He looked small and hurt and confused. I too was confused. But something else was building in my gut and my chest, something I had suppressed for a long time—anger.

The officers took off Jeff's handcuffs and the four of them turned to walk out the door, to their patrol cars. Malvis and Walter stood at the same time and held out their hands as though to stop them.

"Wait a minute!" Malvis said. "You're not going to just leave him here, are you? You've *got* to take him somewhere to get help! He's saying all the right things now and he means them, but this just keeps happening over and over, and his mind's not right! He's not really like this! He would never hurt a fly, not to mention his wife, who he's loved since high school. There's something wrong with him, Officer! He's barely hanging on here, don't you see? He's going to hurt someone, and then he'll hate himself once he gets back to normal. He needs to go somewhere like the state hospital and get treatment!"

"I'm sorry, ma'am, are you his mother?" he said.

"Yes, I'm his mother, and this is not normal for him. There is something wrong in his head. He is sick, and he needs help!" she said.

"I'm sorry, Mrs. Green, but our hands are tied because he did not actually hurt anyone and has never been in trouble with the law before. He no longer poses what we consider a threat to himself or to you, so we can't take him anywhere. I strongly encourage you to get him in to see a doctor, and if they say he needs to be in the hospital, there are procedures they can follow, and then we would have the authority to pick him up and take him. But as it is," the officer said, spreading his hands and shrugging his shoulders as he continued, "there is nothing we can do. But be sure to call if there are any more problems, ma'am, and especially if he hurts anybody," the officer said, and they left.

We sat there, silent and stunned. Even Jeff looked surprised.

CHAPTER 13:

CLARITY

December 1974, San Antonio, Texas

I had not told the police or Jeff's parents about how he held me in the trailer against my will and raped me a few days before, but if they weren't impressed with premeditated attempted murder, I'm not sure it would have made any difference. Besides, I didn't have the language—none of us had the language—to call it rape or kidnapping when such a thing happened between married people, like it was a husband's prerogative. It was dark and nearing bedtime by the time the police left, and I remember calmly unfolding the living room sofa into the sleeper bed where Jeff lay down and was soon fast asleep.

"Susie, why don't you go back and sleep on my bed," Malvis said, "and I'll sleep next to Jeff. He won't bother me."

"No," I said, "I'm going to walk out in the backyard for a bit, and then I'll lay down in here. He's asleep now, and I don't think he'll do anything else. Leave your bedroom door open though."

"I'm going to pray on all this," she said, "and I know you will, too. The Lord will take care of us; you know He will. We just have to pray, have faith, and keep our wits about us. We'll start calling psychiatrists first thing tomorrow morning." She looked at me, expecting agreement, but I just turned and walked out back.

I was not going outside to pray. I was going outside to reflect on what had happened, acknowledge my anger, and accept the fact that I was alone in this ordeal. I fought back a wave of nausea as I examined the implications of what had happened, of what it meant about his mental state. It had not been an impulsive, anger-driven event. In the cold light of day, he had imagined the scene and then set the stage. He had found the knife, which his parents thought they had hidden, for safety, and then searched until he located the whetstone so he could sharpen it to a fine edge. He had hidden the knife under the pillow in a room he had made sure he could lock from the inside. He had composed himself to win my confidence to get me into the back room after his family were all in their bedrooms for the evening. He might be insane, but he was not stupid. He was clever, in fact. And now he was sleeping like a baby, and the authorities seemed to think that was just fine. But it was not fine by me.

I was staggered by the magnitude of Jeff's betrayal of our love, our vows, and our friendship. I wondered if we could ever regain the trust needed to go on. But I also recognized an uglier truth—I felt contempt toward Jeff. Was there nothing he could do to prevent this from happening? I was sorry that he was being destroyed by this illness, but I couldn't shake the feeling that a stronger person could at least acknowledge the need for help. The Bible taught that the man was supposed to be the head of the family, but I was done with that. No more trying to lead from behind.

And I was angry. In fact, I was enraged, and the target of my fury was God. "Have faith. It is all God's will." "When He closes a door, He always opens a window." Really? I had followed Him with all my heart, put my faith and trust in Him, and given up all our worldly possessions to hitchhike around America, seeking His way and praying fervently for a service-filled, 'blessed', peaceful, fulfilling life, not a crazy, scary, erratic one. And, Jeff, the sweet boy I had married, had done the same, perhaps to excess. And where had that gotten us? Where was Jesus and God, our Father, our protector, who had promised to lead us through the valley of the shadow of death, fearing no evil? I had seen evil tonight—it was in the eyes of a God-fearing lunatic who was once my husband. Thanks for nothing.

No, I did not go outside to pray. I went outside to declare that I would no longer pray. How had I let myself travel so far down a path of blind faith, giving up my own agency? I remembered the Sunday school lesson and my horror when God seemed to have shown His true colors with Abraham when He coerced him into taking his only son, Isaac, to the altar. He raised a knife above his trusting son's body, ready to murder him at the Lord's command. Yes, the Lord's angel stayed his hand before slaughter, but at what cost? Is that what I should take from tonight's event? 'Look how much worse it could have been, Susie?' Was that God's miracle, that at the last moment I was spared from being sliced open and left to die in some macabre scene from an Old Testament tragedy? But maybe God was not real; if so, then what an even greater fool I had been. But whether God existed or not was moot now. I was now confident that there was no supernatural force I could count on to provide help.

I felt clarity and single-mindedness settle into me. What was happening to us now was awful and unfair, but I was not going to stand by and let my unborn child and me be victimized by external events. I was glad to be free of my self-imposed blinders and infuriated to realize how much energy I had wasted holding myself back to stay in the dutiful wife lane. It reminded me of how I felt during our hitchhiking days when we accepted a ride so we could all travel together, warm and dry, even though the driver was not really going where we wanted to go. I realized I was done with following someone else's roadmap. I was done with hitchhiking.

I tilted my head back and saw stars twinkling in the cold December night and a luminous sliver of moon approaching the horizon. I appreciated that these celestial bodies were facts, not beliefs. I had not believed that Jesus lived in the moon for a long time, but I still loved the moon and seeing it tonight, as beautiful as ever, gave me hope. With tears streaming down my face for the first time since today's ordeal, I raised my fist to the night sky and roared.

"*Screw you*, if You are there! *I take* control of *my* life now. I am not asking *you* for anything! I do not understand anything about *you*. It's on *me*!"

I went back into the quiet house and lay down on the sofa bed next to Jeff. I felt the baby move, more than the butterfly kisses I had felt at first, now a tiny fist or knee. I told him or her not to fret; her mama was there to protect her, at all costs. The idea of one day holding her in my arms put a smile on my face. I placed extra pillows over my belly and dozed off and on the rest of the night. Malvis and Walter came in to check on us several times, but Jeff slept soundly until early morning.

I awoke with one thought front and center in my mind. "I would be able to kill him if needed."

There was not a speck of doubt in my mind about whether I could do it. I knew that, if he tried to hurt me or the baby again, I would not hesitate to defend myself, even if it meant I had to kill him. Part of me was horrified at this realization, but mostly I accepted it. There was no help coming from above, and the person I thought was my best friend and life partner was gone. The paradigm shift galvanized me, helped me to focus and to embrace the reality that our survival depended on me and the resources I could muster from friends and family. It was a relief in many ways: no more pretending I was less smart or less capable of making my own way in life, no more waiting for the Lord to intervene and save us. I was up to the challenge and even invigorated by it. I felt whole.

I felt like I had faced the truth, and the truth had set me free.

I did not start packing a pistol or anything like that and I still loved Jeff and wanted him safe and well again, but I had perspective. I was careful to never be alone with him and stayed ready to run or pounce. Unfortunately, Jeff had not awakened with a miraculous clarity of mind; quite the opposite, his paranoia and agitation worsened by the hour.

"That's the third psychiatrist's office that has turned us down," I said to Malvis as I walked into the living room. "The last one said they are happy to see Jeff if he will come to the office today between 2:00 and 4:00 p.m., but no, they do not make house calls.

"But the second office's nurse gave me the details of what steps we need to take," I went on. "The easiest is if Jeff is willing to be voluntarily admitted into a mental hospital for a few days . . ."

"That's not going to happen," Walter said.

"Right," I said, "so we have to go the involuntary commitment route. That means a psychiatrist must examine him in person and declare that he's dangerous, that he's likely to hurt somebody or hurt himself. That doctor can then notarize commitment papers, and those papers get approved by a judge. She said that usually happens quickly, within a few hours. Once that happens, the judge issues a warrant for his arrest, and the police or sheriff's department pick him up . . .

"If they can find him!" Malvis said.

"Exactly," I said. "But when they do, they would take him to the San Antonio State Hospital—maybe your own ward, Malvis!—and start treating him. And all these steps have to take place within seventy-two hours, or the whole thing has to start over."

"But how do we get past the first step?" Walter said. "Can't we go visit the doctor instead and tell the psychiatrist what's been happening, how he locked you in a room with a knife? We could get a police report if that would help."

"I asked them that," I said, "but they said because it's such a serious thing, like putting someone in jail, it can't just be based on our stories. The doctor has to witness his craziness, I guess. I begged them; believe me."

"Where's Jeff now?" Malvis asked.

"He came in while Susie was on the phone in the kitchen," Walter said, "figured out that she was talking to someone about him, grabbed a carton of milk from the fridge, and ran out the door again. He's got the keys to the car. I thought I told you to hide them, Malvis!"

"I *did* hide them," she said, offended at his tone. Then she put her hand to her mouth and looked annoyed. "Oh," she said, "that's why he said he needed to use my hairbrush, so he could get in the bedroom. He must have looked in my top drawer and found them. Brother! He might have a screw loose, but he's craftier than ever!"

Later that evening, near dinner time, Jeff came in the house, cautiously.

"Hey, Jeff, come on in, son," Malvis said. "You must be starving. Supper's ready in half an hour. Jeff, look at me—wait. Come here . . ."

He stopped for a moment, turned around, and let his mother come close.

"You remember you told the police that you would go back and see the psychiatrist? We don't want another thing like that to happen, so how about we . . ."

He grinned at her, broke free from her hold, and started loading up a bag with food from the stove and fridge.

"I know what y'all are trying to do, and it's not going to work," he said. "I'm not going to be locked up! I've got work to do. See ya!" He headed for the car and left before we could do more.

Finally, we got a call back from the office of a psychiatrist who made emergency house calls. After several minutes of our explanations, he agreed to help, and we hatched a plan that hinged on Jeff coming back to the house near the next mealtime. The psychiatrist showed up at the agreed-upon time, but Jeff was not there. Nevertheless, he sat with us, writing down all the facts we could provide and examples of recent behavior. Midway through, Jeff burst through the front door, disheveled and wild-eyed. He saw us talking with the stranger sitting on the sofa, turned on his heel, and ran but not before flashing a mischievous, almost gleeful smile as though to say, "Game on!"

Malvis and I threw up our hands in despair and frustration.

"I am so sorry," the psychiatrist said. "I can see this is hard for you all. Listen, we just need to keep trying. I hope he doesn't do anything that gets the police involved before we get commitment papers, but it might come to that. If you think you know where he will be, call this number. My nurse will find me, and hopefully I can get there in time." He handed me a card with a handwritten phone number on it.

Later that day, we had a call from a neighbor.

"Malvis, this is Theresa, next block over. I was calling to say a boy came by today, and I'm pretty sure it's your son, Jeff. He knocked on the door and asked for something to eat and drink. He was acting strange and asked if he could leave some of his things here, and we said that was fine. It was just so odd, I thought I should call and make sure everything was alright."

"Theresa, thank you so much for calling. Here's the situation . . ." Malvis said and briefly explained what was going on. "We desperately need a psychiatrist to see him before we can get him committed to the hospital for treatment. Would it be alright if we came over to your house, with the doctor, and waited for him to show up?"

"Oh, Malvis, I am so sorry that's going on. I had a cousin who had something similar; it is so sad. Of course, y'all come on over, and we'll do what we can to help."

A little while later, the doctor joined us there.

"Hi, I parked down the street, so hopefully Jeff won't recognize the car," the doctor said, coming into the neighbor's house where we sat, waiting. "Can you tell me what he said and what he was like when he came here today?" he asked Theresa.

"Jeff used to be friends with our middle son, so he's not a complete stranger, but he did not act like the boy I used to know; that's for sure," she said. "He seemed worried and nervous and was talking real fast. And he said that someone was chasing him. I guess that would be you?"

It was warm enough that our neighbors left the front door open so we could watch through their screen door for any sign of Jeff's approach. We filled the next half hour telling the doctor (and the neighbor) anecdotes about Jeff's recent mindset and behavior. The doctor took copious notes but eventually declared that he needed to get back to his office where patients were waiting. Just then, Jeff's car pulled up to the curb, and we sat quiet and still as he started walking toward the front door. He stopped midway up the walk and looked around; it was like he smelled that something was afoot. He turned around and ran back to the car, and the psychiatrist rushed to the door and watched him speed off.

"OK, well, it's a stretch, but I can say I 'saw' him, and I certainly have enough evidence to be confident that he needs to be in a hospital at least for an assessment, if not for treatment," the doctor said to our great relief. He signed the commitment papers, and once we got notice that the judge had signed the order and the sheriffs had the warrant, we thought we were home free.

Jeff came back to his parents' house to sleep sometime in the middle of that night. When we awoke and saw him asleep in his old bed the next morning, we called the number they had given us, and within a few minutes the sheriff's officers were there. Tight shirts and bulging bellies, with billy clubs at their sides, they had handcuffs on him before he fully woke up. They walked him past us, out the front door and into the back of their squad car. Jeff looked at me and his mother with such hurt and betrayal that our cries that "It's for your own good" and "We had no other choice" felt empty and mean. It was terribly emotional, and we wept in each other's arms, knowing it was indeed for his own good but feeling awful that he had to be treated like a criminal.

CHAPTER 14

BETTER LIVING THROUGH CHEMISTRY

December 1974 to Spring 1975, San Antonio, Texas

The San Antonio State Hospital was funded by the Texas legislature in 1889, establishing the first public state mental institution to serve southwestern Texas. It was originally known as the Southwestern Insane Asylum. However, in 1925, the word "hospital" was substituted for "asylum" and such adjectives as "insane" and "lunatic" were dropped from most hospital names. We locals still knew it as "the looney bin." All my life I had referred to the place by its street address: South Presa. It was only a fifteen-minute car drive from the house where I grew up and the stuff of taunts and slumber party horror stories.

"I heard her mother was sent to South Presa, she's so crazy!" or "My cousin's best friend was making out in the car with her boyfriend last week when they heard on the radio of an escaped patient from South Presa, an amputee with a hook for a hand. They got worried when they heard something scratching on the door. Her boyfriend started the car and drove off like a bat out of hell! When they got to her home, he went to open her door and there was a bloody hook hanging on the car door handle!" Every town has a focal point for such legends, and the state hospital on South Presa Street was ours. This is where I had just committed my husband for care, against his will but for his own good, I hoped.

It was hours before we could find someone at the hospital who could tell us what ward he had been admitted to and what the plans were. The nurse stated that someone would call us once his intake and assessment were complete. Finally, we got a call.

"Susie, it's me," Jeff cried into the telephone. "Take me home. Please, please, please come get me and take me home. Tell my momma they're trying to kill me, for real. I'll be good; I promise. Please don't leave me here!"

"Jeff, what's going on?" I said. "We thought we were going to hear from the doctors. Did they give you medicine?"

"They held me down like a dog and then gave me a shot in the butt with a huge needle and said I'd feel better soon, but they lied. It was poison! I started twitching and having muscle spasms and then my back arched backwards. I was possessed like no demons I've ever seen before, and I was screaming and finally—"

Jeff's voice cut off and we could hear scuffling and background noise, and then another voice came on the line.

"Hello, who is this?" the voice said.

"This is Jeff's wife! He called me and said something horrible was going on. What's happening? We thought we were going to hear from the doctor by now," I said.

Walter and Malvis had picked up on the extension and were listening as well.

"I am one of the night attendants," he said, "and Mr. Green does not have phone privileges yet, so he shouldn't have called you. The doctor has been very busy tonight, so he hasn't had a chance to call yet, but the social worker may be in touch later. Anyway, unfortunately, Jeff has had a reaction to one of the medications we gave him to calm him down. It happens now and then, and we've given him another injection to counteract it, but he doesn't trust us and is worried we did it on purpose. He'll be fine."

I now know that the reaction he had is called opisthotonos, a painful dystonic reaction seen most often in young men, usually after receiving their first few doses of certain antipsychotics like Thorazine or Haldol. The reaction causes the person to have severe muscle cramps such that their bodies become twisted and contorted until the drug wears off or they are given an antidote like Cogentin.

I had seen the movie *One Flew Over a Cuckoo's Nest*, and all I could think about was Jack Nicholson's character McMurphy and Nurse Ratched. I was beside myself with worry and guilt that he had to endure such a miserable and painful reaction and that he was in such an alien and frightening environment. Fortunately, Malvis was well aware of the type of reaction they were describing and tried to allay my distress, telling me they would get it under control and that the Cogentin would counter its effects. I had worked so hard to get him in the hospital, and now I was filled with anxiety for him.

Jeff was diagnosed with acute paranoid schizophrenia, a form of psychotic mental illness. He was the typical age for onset (usually age sixteen to thirty), and his symptoms were classic. Over the next few days, he went through intensive psychiatric, psychological, and social work evaluations, and I was also interviewed and kept up to date by the social worker who served as the main contact with families. His commitment hearing confirmed that he was to stay under involuntary commitment orders, which had to be revisited and reconfirmed every two to four weeks. Meanwhile, the social worker told us that, though Jeff was under orders for involuntary commitment, the current state hospital medical leadership were proponents of the latest psychiatric trend that encouraged a more open and voluntary approach to treatment, especially for a first-time patient like Jeff. Thus, Jeff was assigned a ward that was unlocked during the day, encouraging patients to take responsibility for their treatment progress and stay there under their own volition. We were distressed but not totally shocked, then, when he walked back to his parents' house a day or two later.

"Jeff, hello! Why are you here? How did you get here?" I said when I saw him walk through the front door. He came over and hugged me and asked if he could eat something and begged me to let him stay. Meanwhile, I could hear Walter on the phone in the back and assumed he was calling the hospital. They didn't even know he was missing, but when they confirmed it, they notified the police. They came and picked him up, but he escaped several more times over the first week or two. Usually, the ward nurse or social worker would call and say he had escaped and that the city police would be on the lookout for him. That would trigger our own search for him, including his parents' and neighbor's yards, cars, and garage. Once we found him sleeping in my dad's camper van outside our old house a few blocks away, but he ran away before the police could apprehend him. Our nerves were frayed, and Jeff took pride in his cunning escapes until finally they decided maybe it was best that he be assigned to a real lockdown unit on the hospital campus. It was clear that the staff were as frustrated as the patients' families with this unworkable theoretical approach. Administrators making such rules had obviously spent little to no time with someone in the throes of acute psychosis.

After Jeff was assigned to the locked ward of the hospital and received an uninterrupted schedule of Haldol, he started improving. Before too long, he was recognizable as the Jeff I had married years ago. He began to recognize that the intrusive thoughts and bullying voices in his head were not heaven sent but classic symptoms of schizophrenia. The pressure he felt to leave his wife and family was the illness talking, not God. The hyper religiosity began to fade, and we talked about more normal things.

But the illness coupled with life on a mental ward had taken a toll on him. The first weekend he had an overnight pass and we slept in the same bed was jarring.

"Jeff," I said, "you smell . . . rank. When's the last time you showered or changed your underwear?"

He saw that I was looking at a brown disgusting smudge of something on the bedsheets where he had been sitting.

"Oh, yeah, I guess you don't know what it's like to be on a mental ward, Susie," he said. He didn't do anything to rectify it, though; he just lay on his side facing away from me and fell to sleep. It was like bringing a feral animal into the house.

By March, he began transitioning to a mostly outpatient basis for treatment. I had been staying with my mother and Jim, but I started spending most of my time at his parents' house until Jeff got a full-time construction job. At that point, we moved into a rental house on San Antonio's south side.

Jeff's sanity was, of course, not the only thing I had to worry about during the fall of 1974 and winter of 1975. I was carrying a full load of senior classes in college, including comparative anatomy and its lab, and a chemistry research seminar. The term continued even as my husband's mind, and any semblance of normality in my life, collapsed. When Christmas break was about to commence, I knew I was in academic jeopardy. I had not finished my chemistry research independent studies project and knew I would not be able to graduate in May unless I completed it. I had never been in this circumstance in my life, and I was mortified. I made an appointment to see my advisor and chemistry professor, Dr. Ray Rataiczak. In looks he reminded me of the actor William Shatner of *Star Trek* fame, and like Captain Kirk, he was someone you did not want to disappoint. I had given him a folder showing the status of my project a few days earlier.

We sat in Dr. Ray's tiny book-crammed office, and he looked at me, looked at the folder, and then back at me, shaking his head side to side.

"Carol," he said, "to say I'm disappointed in you is an understatement. And surprised! I never imagined I would see you so unprepared. Do you have any credible reason for your failure to get this done?"

My face was beet red and hot with embarrassment. I remember sitting there with my head bent in shame, barely able to talk without breaking into sobs, accepting responsibility while also summarizing the hell I had been living the past several months. I accepted a Kleenex from him without looking up.

"Also," I said, finishing my tale of woe, "I'm four months pregnant. But the good news is that the intense fatigue of the first trimester is less than it was a few weeks ago, and thank goodness I am not having morning sickness. I hope now that my husband is locked up and being treated in the mental hospital, I can make up my work if you and my other seminar teachers would please give me an extension.

"I'm so sorry and embarrassed that I disappointed you and all my teachers," I croaked and then blew my nose. I heard only silence and finally looked up to see tears flowing down Dr. Ray's cheeks. He leaned over, put his elbows on his knees, and took both of my hands in his.

"Carol, child, why didn't you come talk to me, or one of us, weeks ago? Carol, my God, what you have been through! I had no idea. None of us did. Oh, my goodness. And you're pregnant on top of everything. Of course, you will have an extension. I will talk to the other faculty, and I'm sure they will agree."

When I returned to school after the Christmas break, Dr. Rataiczak and my other teachers made a point to check in on Jeff's progress along with my pregnancy and emotional state while giving full academic support; plus, my professors who were also nuns started praying for me. I completed my work over the next few weeks and was cleared for finishing my senior year of college, to include student teaching biology at a local high school. I wished I had confided in them earlier, and I will always be grateful for how they stood by me during some very difficult days.

Then there was the issue of money. We had none. Thus, in addition to help from our parents, I applied for public assistance and received food stamps and free pre-natal and obstetric care at Robert B. Green, San Antonio's public maternity hospital. Like my peers, I was in favor of all things organic and natural and hoped to be able to deliver the baby with as little medical intervention as possible. I was also adamant about nursing my baby and read extensively about both natural childbirth and breastfeeding.

The "granola" movement was well under way in 1975, and Lamaze classes for natural childbirth in hospital as well as lay midwife-supervised home deliveries were becoming popular. During the intake session at the Robert B. Green hospital, they mentioned that, if I preferred, rather than being assigned to the resident doctor's clinic, I could be a patient of their certified nurse midwife. Certified specialty-trained nurse midwives were new to American hospitals, but I immediately said yes, hoping she would work with me rather than patronize me like the first doctor I saw. Plus, I had already been told about her by my friend Kathy, so I was glad to come under the care of Ms. Joan Hoffmaster. She became an essential part of the support team I needed to make it through Jeff's illness and my pregnancy.

"Good morning, Carol," Ms. Hoffmaster said during our January visit. "You look well but tired. What's been going on since I saw you last month?" "Do you think babies are affected by adrenaline?" I asked her. "Because if so, this baby is going to pop out ready to run an Olympic race!" I unloaded the recent events, including being threatened at knife point and Jeff's commitment to the mental hospital. My visits with her became a critically important lifeline for my mental health. She was concerned about the stress I was under, especially when my blood pressure started to rise to an unacceptable level.

"Carol," she said, "I'm going to ask one of the doctors to examine you today. This is the third month in a row that your blood pressure has been high, and I believe you are developing preeclampsia."

Hypertension that emerges during pregnancy can be the harbinger of a serious condition called preeclampsia, which can lead to full blown eclampsia resulting in seizures and death for the mom and baby, if untreated. The best treatment, in that case, is immediate delivery of the baby. Thus, our main goal was to keep my blood pressure under control until the baby was mature enough for a healthy delivery.

The house had one bathroom and two bedrooms. The kitchen had a washing machine, which was a godsend for all the diapers I eventually had to launder. The backyard was fenced, and there was a small garage around the back. My mom and mother-in-law, girlfriends, aunts, and cousins gave us a baby shower, so we had lovely handmade blankets and all the necessary baby paraphernalia to make the nursery room look and smell wonderful.

At last, I thought, *I can put away the baby shower gifts and get the crib set up and figure out where the changing table will be . . .*

But shortly after we moved in, my intense need to start "nesting" was thwarted by the strict bed rest Ms. Hoffmaster placed me on owing to worsening high blood pressure. Fortunately, my mother was there to help me, and together we organized the house and set up the nursery, including the beautiful baby crib that she and Dad bought for us.

I was so bored and frustrated with having to lie on my left side for days on end that the idea of washing and drying dishes in my kitchen sounded like heaven. To add insult to injury, I had no sign that I was ready to deliver on my due date, and I was forbidden to attend my college graduation ceremony for fear of tipping into preeclampsia. My blood pressure kept creeping up, and by May 20, they broke the placental membranes to induce labor, and then added a Pitocin drip to speed things up. I labored hard and exhaustingly with Jeff and my mom taking turns at my side and Ms. Hoffmaster carefully monitoring me and consulting the doctors about my lack of progress. After about twenty hours, it became clear that, as the first obstetrician had predicted, my pelvis was too flat to allow the baby to be delivered normally. I underwent a Cesarean section that night, and my beautiful healthy daughter was born.

In 1975, the childbirth experience in the US was still extremely medicalized and controlled by doctors, predominately men, and older nurses. In San Antonio, at least, they were not at the vanguard of patient autonomy or experiential childbirth. My first memory after the general anesthesia for Cesarean section is of a recovery room nurse holding my arm and preparing to inject something into my IV line.

"*Stop*," I said, groggy but definite. "What are you giving me?" I had nearly died from an antibiotic drug allergy as a child and was hyperalert about knowing what someone was about to feed me or inject into me.

"Don't you worry about it, honey. It's just something to dry up your milk," she said.

Now truly awake, I pulled my arm away from her.

"*No*, I don't want anything to dry up my milk. I plan to breastfeed my baby!" I said.

She looked at me in surprise but was adamant.

"Now give me your arm, dear," she said. "The doctor has ordered it, and if you don't cooperate, I'll have to call him!"

"Call him if you want, but it's my body, my baby, and my decision! *No drug* to dry up my milk!" I said. "And bring me a blanket! I'm so cold!"

She huffed and puffed and paged the doctor who, to her annoyance, told her it was alright if I refused the medicine. Wow!

I felt my only ally in the medical system was Ms. Hoffmaster who obviously could not be at my bedside every minute. Unfortunately, I developed a fever, which meant IV antibiotics. But even worse, they would not let me hold my baby until I was fever free for twenty-four hours and could not breastfeed until the antibiotics had been stopped. When Ms. Hoffmaster came by to see me the evening after the 2:00 a.m. birth of my child, she chided the nursing staff for not helping me get up all day. She then took it upon herself to get me into a wheelchair and push me and my IV pole out of the six-woman ward to the newborn nursery. I looked at my daughter through the nursery's glass window, as though I was any other visitor, and saw that she was the most beautiful baby ever. I went back to my bed, thanked Ms. Hoffmaster for her help and kindness, pulled the covers over my head, and cried. I was beside myself with the need to hold and feed my baby. Eventually they let me hold her, but initially I was only allowed to feed her formula from a bottle while the antibiotics were finishing up. She kept spitting out the nipple and screwing up her face at the concoction. The nurses declared that she did not seem to be a "good eater."

There was no such thing as keeping the baby next to the mother's bedside at that hospital, at that time; all babies stayed in the nursery unless they were being fed. When I was given the green light to go ahead with breastfeeding and taking instructions from my La Leche League dog-eared book I had been studying, I asked the nurses to stop all formula and water feedings and bring her to me as soon as she started crying. They ignored my request the first time, such that she was full of baby formula and just slept when they brought her to me, but I repeated my request more forcefully, and when the night nurse finally brought her to me, she was hungry, for sure. When I held her in my arms and she got her first taste of real mother's milk, I swear she looked up at me with a look that said, "Now, see, *that's* what I'm talking about!" Anyway, that's how I remember it, and she was a plenty good eater!

We finally got home, and like any new parents, we were anxious whether we were doing things right and not at all certain that she would breathe if we weren't looking at her every minute. Though she loved the breastmilk, she did not love sleeping. The first six weeks were hard for me, still recovering from surgery and being the only one with "the goods" that could nourish and comfort her.

My mother and father were also making changes in their lives while we were welcoming a baby into our home. Having rekindled their love for each other during clandestine meetings, they gave each other the strength to end their other marriages, live independently, and figure out if they could make a life together again. My mom had recently moved into her own apartment and could come and go as she wished, without having to face Jim's whining or recriminations. It was a relief to have her with me from breakfast to supper time every day for the first week, helping with the cooking, cleaning up, and laundry while I focused on the baby. She also gave me what every new mother craves—an hour to bathe or shower or nap alone, with complete confidence that all is well with the child! And Mom loved bonding with her new granddaughter, the new light of her life.

There are sweet memories from those first months of parenthood. The baby was the absolute center of our attention. Though we named her April Nicole, we called her Nikki from the start. She had loads of reddish-brown hair that stood up in a way that reminded me of Woody Woodpecker's. I remember being in awe that my body could make such nutritious and obviously delicious milk; after the first few gulps, her little eyes would roll back in her head like she was in ecstasy. It was her drug, her opiate, her heart's desire! And in such quantities, it was like she was drinking from a little fire spout! I took to capturing the extra milk with a hand-held small plastic breast pump so I could freeze it and let Mom or Jeff take turns with the feeding.

I set up a baby jump seat in the hallway door, and once she was old enough, Nikki would go berserk using her little chubby legs to jump up and down, up and down, until Jeff would walk through the front door, home from work. Hearing the door, she would come to a standstill, focus on his face as he grinned at her, and they would both erupt into giggles. Other times he would put her up on his shoulders and walk around until she laid her head on the top of his and went to sleep.

A pair of cardinals built a nest in an evergreen bush planted outside in the corner of the house where our bedroom joined the nursery, and I delighted in their diligence at parenting and daily monitored the progress of the eggs and then nestlings. They were building their family, just like we were. Life seemed to be bursting out everywhere, and I fervently wanted to believe our troubles were behind us.

I sobbed unconsolably when we woke one day to find the nest knocked out of the bush and on the ground, fledglings gone, clumps of feathers strewn about.

CHAPTER 15

MADNESS STOPS FOR NOTHING

Summer 1975, San Antonio, Texas

Jeff and I were living the dream for three to four months, like a happy, normal family. Jeff had no problem with diaper duty, having done it plenty of times as a big brother to his three younger siblings and nephew in years past, and he adored his daughter. He went to work on a construction job during the week, went fishing or otherwise tromping around in the woods with his brothers on the weekend, and started a garden in the backyard of our rental house. We had friends and family who dropped by, and we went to our parents' homes often.

Jeff seemed back to normal and even had a playful sense of humor again. But my worry that his psychotic break might not have been a one-time occurrence lingered.

"Hey, Jeff, you got this letter from the psychiatry clinic today," I said from the kitchen. Jeff had cleaned up after work and was lying on the rug in the living room next to Nikki who was on her own quilt, feet up in the air, gnawing on her favorite yellow toy giraffe. He was doing something that made her giggle every minute or two. I walked in from the kitchen where I was working on supper and watched them. The scene made me very happy.

"Did you hear me?" I said. "It's there on the coffee table. It says you've missed two appointments. That makes me kind of nervous, hon." He didn't say anything but just kept entertaining the baby.

"I thought they needed to see you every month to make sure the pills are working like they should and not causing any problems," I said. No response.

"You're still taking the pills they sent you home with, aren't you?" I asked. After a minute, Jeff stood and, letting out a big sigh, scooped up Nikki and sat down in the rocking chair with her. He cradled her in his lap, making sure the giraffe was still in her grasp.

"I didn't pick up last month's pills," he said. "Maybe the last two months. I hate them, Susie. They make me feel like I'm dead. Except that they also make my skin crawl, and I can't sit still; remember I had to rock back and forth constantly? It's a horrible feeling. And I'm groggy after I take them and then wired a few hours later. I feel so much better off of them."

"Have you had any of those scary voices or thoughts in your head?" I asked.

"No, nothing. Everything seems normal and good. I think I just need to be careful and not get too deep into philosophical or religious things, you know? And just get on with life. And besides, how can I be crazy with this little girl needing all these kisses?" he said as he started giving her tickly kisses down her neck, tummy, and toes.

I sympathized with him. I had witnessed the incessant rocking he could not control and the glazed look in his eyes when he was on the pills in the hospital and for weeks after. And now that I thought about it, perhaps his getting completely back to normal coincided with him getting off the pills. So, I did not put up much of a fuss. The doctors had not included me in any conversations about what to expect in the long run, and at least one of the doctors had said that sometimes a schizophrenic break only happens once. I seemed to remember that the famous singer James Taylor had been in a mental hospital, and last I heard, he was fine. Jeff was so much back to normal now and seemed happy to move on, as was I. Surely it was all behind us.

My friend Kathy and I hadn't seen each other much during our pregnancies but talked by phone and delivered our babies within a few weeks of each other, same hospital and same nurse midwife. Since this was Kathy's third child, she was a great support during my early breastfeeding days. Now we were sitting in my backyard sipping tea, hers with lemon just the way I knew she liked it, exchanging updates on sleeping patterns, diaper rashes, and developmental milestones.

"How's Jeff doing?" she asked. "Everything good?"

"I guess so," I said. "He pretty much seems like the old Jeff, though there are subjects we avoid, like we don't talk about church or God or religion, and we don't really talk about what happened when he was in the depths of . . . craziness."

"But . . .?" she said.

"I just found out that he isn't taking the pills anymore," I said, "and he stopped going to his psychiatry appointments. I never got a clear idea from the doctors how important it was for him to keep taking the pills, but I know he hates the side effects, and I don't want to force the issue. He seems just as happy to be living a normal life as I am. He loves playing with Nikki, and you see the garden he is preparing?"

Photo 11: Kathy and I with our infants, summer 1975.

She sipped her tea and appraised the large expanse of tilled earth in the back corner of the yard. Jeff had already created the rows for planting. The babies were on blankets in the grass in front of us, both awake now, cooing and babbling, playing with their own toes and fingers, and occasionally noticing each other.

"He's got a decent job," I said, "and we have friends and family close by. I hope all that is enough to let his mind permanently heal. But what about you? Is Benito working?" I said. "More importantly, is he drinking?"

Unfortunately, he was drinking hard again, and she wasn't sure what to do about it. For now, she needed to stay focused on her infant son and other two boys and hope things would improve.

"I keep meaning to ask," I said, "whatever happened to that car, the red Barracuda we left with you when we headed off to Abilene?"

"Oh, it ran great for another nine months," she said. "It was a godsend while I finished that last year of med tech internship out at Bexar County hospital. But then it developed a problem with the transmission, I think it was," she said, "and my brother-in-law got a good deal on a newer car—also a Barracuda but this one blue—and so we traded it in. I drove that one the next year and then you-know-who got out of prison, and I got pregnant and a few months ago the 'new' car was a casualty of one of his drinking binges. It's fixable, and I know where it is, but no one's gotten around to getting a tow truck to pick it up and get it running again. Since I'm home with the baby and not working, I just use my mother-in-law's car if I can't get there on the bus."

"You know," she said after a few minutes, "I think it just needs some body work and basic repairs, and if you thought Jeff or your dad wanted to get it up and running, you could have a car at home when Jeff is off at work," she said.

"Interesting idea," I said. "Let me check with Dad and Jeff and see what they say."

A week or two later, Dad and I went to check out the car and then had it towed to our house. Dad came over on weekends, and soon enough I had a functional car to use when Jeff was at work. Normally Jeff would have helped as well, but oddly he did not seem to have much interest in the project.

A few weeks later Kathy called and confided that her family situation was deteriorating.

"He's almost never sober now," she said, "and I can't raise the boys like this. But he will never agree to a divorce," she said, "and if he knows I'm going to try to leave anyway, he'll cause a ruckus. And the boys will not like the idea of leaving their dad, no matter what," she told me.

"Where are you going to move to? Won't he track you down?" I asked.

"I've been talking to my mom, and she's ready for us to move back home to Montana and stay with her, so that's no problem. And it's far enough away that, without a functioning car of his own, he's unlikely to get there without us having plenty of warning. Mom sent me an open-date plane ticket. I just need to figure out when and how to get to the airport and airborne before he suspects anything," she said.

"Is there a plan? Anything I can do to help?" I asked.

"Yeah, I think so. I've been talking to my mother-in-law. She hates the idea that she won't see her grandsons growing up but agrees that something must give," Kathy said. I knew that she and Kathy were very close, and the boys would miss being with their beloved abuela.

"We think next week is a good time," she said, "when he meets with his parole officer and goes to support group. He will be gone long enough for us to get out of the house and to the airport. It's soon, but that's OK because my oldest already has a feeling something is going on and he's on edge. We have to keep plans secret from him because he's so conflicted, being defensive about his father while protective of me," Kathy went on.

"Can I drive you to the airport? Dad and I have the blue Barracuda up and running, and I could leave the baby with my mother-in-law," I suggested, nervous about a potential confrontation but anxious to help her escape. We settled on the details and made our arrangements.

On the agreed-upon day, I left Nikki with Malvis and drove to Kathy's home where she had the kids packed up and ready to go. The older boy had seen the packed suitcases and was fretful and anxious. With tearful goodbyes, the boys hugged their abuela, and we sped off to the airport. They made it safely to their new lives, first in Montana, and later in Colorado, where Kathy raised her three sons while going back to school to become a pediatric advanced practice practitioner. She worked in clinics that served all members of the community, with a special sensitivity to the needs of immigrant and low-income populations. She has remained an activist for justice in the US and abroad her entire life and is an active participant in the lives of her children and grandchildren. Her ex-husband sadly died of alcoholic liver disease when the boys were still growing up.

Kathy and I were there for each other when it counted, in ways that made a difference. We had become strong women and did not want to accept defeat or mediocrity. When necessary, we put our family on our shoulders and plowed ahead— get on board or get out of the way. But while Kathy was getting her life back on track, mine was about to go off the rails again.

I remember vividly the first conversation to herald Jeff's return to madness. It seemed innocuous, kind of ridiculous really. Jeff and I were sitting in the living room after supper; I was nursing the baby and getting ready to put her into bed when he said, "I've been thinking about climbing mountains. I read in *National Geographic* the other day that men are climbing Mount Everest without sherpas now. Doesn't that sound far out? Climbing the highest mountain with nothing but your own strength and planning and courage! That's what I want to do. That's what I'm going to do," he said.

The idea was so out of his league and the comment so out of the blue that I laughed it off, saying something like, "Sure, and I think I'll sign up as an astronaut next week and go to the moon."

Jeff was strong and fit, and he could have been a rock or mountain climber if he had prepared for it, but he had never shown an ounce of interest in such a thing. I knew for a fact that he had no technical climbing skills, and I had read enough to know that Sir Edmund Hilary did not just decide one week to climb the highest peak in the world, fly over to Kathmandu, and sally up the mountain.

Jeff turned angry and derisive, asking, "Well, what is your ambition? Is this all you want to do with the rest of your life, sit in a rocking chair with a baby at your breast? How can you *not* want to climb a mountain?

What kind of a bloodsucker are you, just to want to live off my paycheck? Don't you want to achieve something greater?"

I blinked. "You might have noticed that just a few months ago I had a baby," I said, "who I am full-time mothering right now! I am happy to be past the pain of a Cesarean section, the nightmare of schizophrenia, and now getting a few hours of sleep each night. That kind of feels like a mountain, to me. And you are playing a huge role in all this by making sure your family has the food and shelter needed to grow and be healthy. Why is that not another kind of amazing mountain to tackle?

"And what makes you think you can go climb Mount Everest?" I said. "You've never climbed anything taller than a telephone pole!" I exclaimed, worked up by now. "Why don't you aspire to a more realistic goal like finishing college and becoming a forest ranger, which you always said you wanted to do?" I asked, getting down to what I thought were some real issues we should address.

Once he was asleep, my mind was roiling with the injustice of his words. I felt a first rush of feminist indignation.

Typical of men to push aside the birth and rearing of a child as "nothing," I thought, relegating the care and feeding of the family to a category much less than "greatness." Women are less often in the history books because they are up to their necks in putting food on the table, cleaning and organizing the men and children so they can succeed, ministering to the husband's sexual needs (and her own if she's lucky), and then bearing his children. When women do something momentous, they take it in stride; men spend the rest of their lives crowing about it. Men plant flags atop the mountains, while women jump thousands of foot-high hurdles between sunup and sundown for their families. Men have sponsors and teams that pay them to carry, hit, or kick a ball, run, ski, swim, or fly faster and farther. Women live in shadows, sometimes in economic bondage to their menfolk, keeping the lights on, the school fees paid, and the clothes mended and cleaned.

The argument was our first since his discharge from the hospital and could have signaled a return to real normalcy where husbands and wives hammer out ideas and opinions, grand and mundane, hopefully with humor and respect. But I soon realized that my righteous indignation was covering up a growing concern. Like whistling in the dark, I was distracting myself from the clanging alarm bells signaling "Here we go again!" It was not that the idea of mountain climbing was insane; it was the grandiosity of the idea juxtaposed with the contempt he threw at me that raised my hackles.

We did not dwell on the argument, and I kept whistling, hoping the alarm bells were false. But Jeff became increasingly controlling and paranoid and every few days had some other elaborate and unrealistic notion, though they did not return to a focus on God or Satan. Once again, I found myself trying to placate, mollify, and deflect his ideas, but I did not try to hide my concern from him or our families. We all needed to be aware and alert, and I needed them to be on board. We encouraged him to check in with the mental health clinic and consider getting back on the medications, but he said the psychiatrists were the crazy ones and had nothing to offer other than drugs that took away his soul. He became more and more distracted when he was home and less interested in playing with the baby. His brothers tried to engage him with local hunting or fishing trips, but on the weekends, he would go out alone.

Photo 12: My dad visiting our house and enjoying his granddaughter. Jeff is in the background looking over the garden he had tilled.

One weekend day, Nikki and I returned from visiting Mom at her apartment to find Jeff sitting on the closed commode in our tiny white-tiled bathroom with a shoe box full of our photos on his lap. A small pile of them were burning among other charred bits in the bathroom sink.

"Jeff, what in the world are you doing?" I exclaimed, prepared to reach in and rescue what remained unburnt. But what I saw in his eyes and his demeaner stopped me cold. I registered that he hadn't shaved or bathed in a few days, and he looked at me with anger and accusation, completely ignoring the baby I was still holding in her car seat.

"Get out! Get out!" he said. "I know why you keep these pictures locked away, Susie. *This* is how you can control me! You're all getting fat, sucking the life out of me!"

I went to the nursery, lifted the baby out of her car carrier, placed her in the crib for safety, and then ran to the bathroom. I was desperate to try to save the photos, upset that he was destroying so many precious mementoes of our lives. He held me at arm's length, pushed me out the bathroom door, and locked himself inside so he could continue feeding the pictures into the makeshift fire. I was angry and frustrated, but I also grieved for Jeff, realizing that one day he would be even sadder than I that he had destroyed evidence of our love and our lives together.

I paced outside the bathroom, talking to him, trying to calm him down, appeal to his reason, and get him to engage with me. But he was silent. Eventually he came out of the bathroom holding the shoebox under his arm.

"Don't try to follow me! You'll never find them!" he said and then got in the car and left with what I assumed was a box of ashes.

Well, there it is, I thought. *No mystery. I've been down this road before.*

My priority was the safety of my daughter and myself. As soon as Jeff left the house, I called my mother to let her know what was happening, packed a suitcase and Nikki's diaper bag, got in the trusty blue Barracuda, and left the house. It would be too dangerous for us to be with him while I engineered his next hospital commitment.

After burning the photos and leaving our house, Jeff ended up back at his parents' house. The next day, after Nikki and I were safely ensconced at my mother's apartment, I went to his parents' house to try to figure out how to get him into care again.

"Malvis, where's Jeff?" I called out when I got there and couldn't find him. She came in from the backyard, flush with frustration and annoyance.

"He's run off!" she said, shaking her head. "I was just looking down the alley to see if I could see him back there. We hid all the car keys, but he ran off cackling like a hen, with something in his hand he said he was trying to bury."

"The ashes from our pictures . . ." I said.

"No, he already buried those in the backyard, and the dog already found them and dug 'em up. It's something else; I don't know what. But I've got a call into the doctor he was supposed to be seeing in the clinic," she said.

"Good!" I said and went outside to search for Jeff.

I finally caught up with him down the block but was taken aback when he walked up to me grinning, dried blood on his lips and face.

"Jeff, honey, what happened? Why is there blood on your face? Are you hurt?" I asked and reached out to touch him. He widened his gap-toothed grin and backed away, dropping a pair of pliers at my feet.

"Don't worry; this is going to help," he said and showed me the bloody remnants of a tooth in the palm of his hand. "They were getting in through here, and they're really mean this time, telling me all sorts of . . . bad things. But that's the end of that!"

"But that's the tooth with the crown, Jeff. Where are you taking it? You were so happy to have gotten it fixed a few months ago . . ." I stood there and watched him run down the street and around the corner before picking up the pliers he'd dropped. I felt nauseated when I saw his blood and grasped the level of mental anguish he must be experiencing to conclude that pulling out his own tooth would be less painful than living with the voices.

My poor, sick husband.

CHAPTER 16

A SOCIAL WORKER'S LIFE-SAVING ADVICE

Fall 1975, San Antonio, Texas

It was much easier to get him committed the second time because he had a known diagnosis of schizophrenia and documented lapse of clinic visits and medication pick-ups. When we got the commitment papers signed and the cops picked him up, we knew better than to let our guards down, and sure enough, he walked out of the facility more than once before being back on the medications and stabilized.

We knew the drill, so at least the ward itself and the processes were less shocking to him and to us. Many of the staff and even some patients were familiar. Though he was not completely freaked out about the place, he did not like it and did not want to be there. He was more belligerent this time and had a new array of strange ideas, many of which he never let go of even when the medications started kicking in. He had decided, for example, that he was getting skinny, and I was getting fat (not true, except when I was pregnant and nursing "fat") because I was somehow siphoning off his weight, like Jack Spratt, I suppose. This idea resurfaced for quite a while, and later when he declared he had a girlfriend at the hospital, I noted that she was obese and he was also gaining weight. When I mentioned it to Jeff, he said something like, "Yeah, I decided to turn the tables, and now she feeds me."

My hopes for a normal life were now shattered. I moved our things out of the small rental house on Steve's Avenue, took Jeff's things to his parents' house, and Nikki and I moved into my mother's apartment. My dreams of staying at home with my daughter as a full-time mom no longer made sense, but I was not ready to leap into a full-time job away from her, especially with Jeff's outcome so much in limbo. Mom and I looked in the newspaper want ads for reasonable job opportunities. I interviewed with several people, including a woman named Carolyn who lived in a north San Antonio suburb. She was looking for a live-in nanny to care for her four children ages three to eleven years old while she finished her master's degree in social work counseling. She was in the process of divorce from her husband.

Carolyn hired me, and we hit it off right away. She was delighted to have a baby back in the house and happy that she was getting a college-educated young mother to care for her children. Nikki and I lived in a bedroom-bathroom suite off the main family room, which also had an entry door from the outside so we could come and go as we pleased. It was a comfortably large space, with room for Nikki's baby crib, the changing table, a bed for me, and my sewing machine. We were instantly enveloped in their messy, loud, wonderful, warm, and lively family. Nikki adored all of them, crawling along the tile floors, eating whatever the kids or their two large dogs left behind if I did not get there soon enough, and playing among the pots and pans in the kitchen while I cooked. Each day I cleaned, learned to yell (at the kids, the dogs, and the world), hugged, tickled, and tucked in all our kids for naps and meals and cried when I felt like it. Carolyn was the first Jewish person I had ever personally known. "Hadn't they gotten the memo?" about Jesus I remember asking her, still more or less thinking that all the Jews had converted once Jesus was born. She helped me understand some about Judaism and Jewish culture and traditions, though she did not keep a Kosher household and did not consider herself religious. Many evenings after the kids were tucked away, we sat on the sofa sharing life stories, disappointments, and hope for the future. We became good friends. Another strong woman was in my life and gave me critical support at a pivotal moment.

Mom and Dad had divorced their respective spouses and bought a house together in northeastern San Antonio. On Friday evenings, Nikki and I would pack a bag and go stay with my parents, arriving back at Carolyn's late Sunday afternoon. It was an incredible relief to have them together again and for us to have a home base, because Jeff 's rehospitalization in the winter and spring of 1976 was long and hard. There was no three-week miraculous breakthrough to the rational young man he had been before. It was more like grinding away at the demons rather than a casting out. He resented the psychiatric and medication intrusion more than the first time and seemed more comfortable now in his scrambled brain than in the medicated more-sane brain. He was less compliant in group and individual therapy and was also comfortable showing me that he was angry, viewing me as his jailer. He only grudgingly accepted that the medicated state, which did not include the insistent, scary voices, was better than the former state and never completely bought in to the treatment plan nor got back to himself.

We were assigned a different ward social worker, and she was determined to make sure we both understood what the future held for us. During our first session with her, she was blunt.

"Jeff," she said, "this is your second psychotic break within the year, and you abandoned all treatment once you switched to outpatient status after the first go-around. I hate to tell you, but we consider that a worrisome sign for the future. Has your doctor told you that?"

Jeff was rocking back and forth, a side effect of the powerful anti-psychotic medications, and smoking one cigarette after another in her office. She was probably smoking, too, common practice in those days.

"Yeah, I guess so," he said.

"Mrs. Green," she said, "the doctors think Jeff is likely to have the chronic version of schizophrenia, which means he will probably have intermittent periods of sanity and insanity the rest of his life. The better he is about staying on the medications, essentially forever, and staying connected with his doctor in clinic, the less often he'll have to be hospitalized for full-blown episodes. You have a child together, is that right?"

"Yes, she's not quite six months old," I said.

"Your safety and your family's safety must be your primary concern, Mrs. Green," she said, and then looked from me to Jeff. "Isn't that right, Jeff?" she said. "You know this illness sometimes has you thinking the unthinkable, right? Have you had the conversation with your family about locking up all guns, knives, and large blunt instruments for now and to always be careful lest you get hold of them when you're in one of these dark places?"

Of course I remembered the locked bedroom and Jeff threatening me with a Bowie knife but had not fully appreciated the need for prospective constant vigilance. I looked at her and then over at Jeff who looked dazed from the heavy doses of drugs but also a little sheepish as though he too had been thinking about getting hold of such objects over the past few weeks. She got him to agree that in his healthy mind he would never want to harm us and that of course we should secure such items. After a bit, she dismissed him, saying she needed to discuss billing and other issues with me. He shuffled out of the room, looking straight ahead and not at me.

"What is your plan, Carol?" she said.

"About what?" I asked.

"About your marriage to Jeff. Have you considered separating from him? Or divorce?"

"No, of course not," I said. "He's my husband, to have and to hold, and all that."

"Have you thought about what it's going to be like to raise a child, and possibly future children, with a chronically mentally ill dad?" "Not really," I said, "but I have been worrying about whether the condition might be inherited. Can you recommend some books to read?"

"Sure," she said, "but one risk factor for schizophrenia is to grow up in the household where one of the parents has schizophrenia. So, just think about that." She leaned forward. "But the most important thing I hope you will get clear in your head is to know that you have rights."

"What do you mean I have rights? Like what?" I asked.

"A right to declare what you expect from Jeff," she said, "and under what conditions you will accept him back to your side, to continue as your husband and your daughter's father."

"Such as 'don't be crazy again'? I don't think he's doing it on purpose, though sometimes it does seem that way," I said.

"No, he cannot help the fact that he has the illness," she said, "but he can choose to take the medications or not. He can choose to work with his doctors to lessen the side effects; he can choose to keep clinic appointments on schedule so we can monitor him for worsening signs and symptoms of the illness, like more frequent intrusive thoughts or auditory or visual hallucinations. When he is clear minded, he can make sure you and your daughter are safe and know what to do in case of emergencies. He can choose to understand his illness and work with us, not against us, to manage it. We have people who mostly live in the community with their families because they work with us and we help them manage it. But this only works if the person accepts what is going on and what it takes to help themselves and their families stay safe and together." She paused and made a few notes before continuing.

"Jeff will vote with his feet," she said. "His actions will speak for themselves. You must decide how you will respond to his actions, his decisions. I strongly advise that you figure out what you can live with and what you refuse to accept, and then make this very clear to Jeff. You need to figure out your own path and try to bring him to you."

The social worker's advice was pivotal. She gave me permission to articulate my boundaries and needs and to set my own course accordingly. She validated my worth and right to set limits to provide safety and security for my family. Jeff could decide to come with me or not, but I did not have to be dragged along unwillingly according to his or anyone else's agenda. I took her advice to heart and discussed the implications with her over multiple sessions while Jeff was an inpatient. I also started verbalizing my expectations to Jeff as he improved.

Photo 13: Nikki and I visiting Jeff at the State Hospital during his second hospitalization.

Once he was more stable and given grounds privileges, I brought Nikki with me to the large state hospital's grounds where we spread a blanket and ate a picnic lunch while she crawled in his lap and across the grass. His parents and siblings visited as well, and, of course, his mother still worked part time on a different ward. She would stop by before or after her shifts and bring him something special to eat or to read. He was starting to look more like himself and had better personal hygiene. But even when he wasn't dazed from the drugs or rocking or pacing from their side effects, our conversation was stilted and unnatural. He was living in a world much different than mine. I fed him the details of our lives, Nikki's new accomplishments, my hopes and fears, trying to get him to come back to normalcy, but it was not happening as easily as the first time. He would tell me about antics on the ward featuring himself or other patients, but they seemed frightening and sad, not funny and mischievous like he made them out to be.

Eventually he started getting day passes, and his parents would pick him up for a day at home where Nikki and I would meet him for a few hours on weekends. We started allowing him to come to Carolyn's house on scheduled visits during daylight hours when we felt comfortable with his state of mind and our ability to get help if needed.

However, one night during the transition phase, he became every parent's worst nightmare.

It was the middle of the night when I was startled awake in our room at Carolyn's house. I did not know what woke me. But running on pure instinct, I dashed to the crib, and hardly conscious, I swooped Nikki up and into my arms. As I did so, I yelped in surprise, as I realized someone was standing there at her crib side reaching for her as well.

"*Stop!*" I screamed. "Who are you? Oh my God, is it you, Jeff?" I realized as I hugged her close to me and turned on a lamp.

"It ain't no big deal, Susie. It's just me and I wanted to see my daughter; nothing wrong with that, is it?" he said, trying to take her from me as I turned away, shielding her. It was 2:00 a.m., and I was angry and scared.

"Get out of here, Jeff!" I yelled at him. "What are you doing here? How did you get in? You are obviously AWOL from your day pass!" I continued. "We're going to call the police and you had better just get away from here right now!"

As intended, the ruckus woke Carolyn who immediately understood what was going on and called the sheriff's department. She barged in through my door, her kids trailing behind dragging blankies and sucking thumbs, wide-eyed at the commotion.

"*Get out!*" she yelled, pointing to the side door where he had entered. "The sheriff's department is on the way!"

"It's none of your business!" Jeff said. "This is *my* wife and *my* daughter, and I don't have to go anywhere!" he declared, belligerently, but no longer reaching for Nikki. She started rooting around to try nursing, and the kids began crying to be held as Carolyn and I stared him down, willing the sirens and bright lights to show up, which they soon did. Jeff tried to evade the sheriff's men, but they corralled him, put him in one of their cruisers, and drove him back to the hospital.

After weeks of medication and more stable behavior, I took Nikki and spent more weekend time at his parents' house when he was there, but I soon figured out that he was skipping medications on the days he was home.

"Jeff, where are your pill bottles?" I asked him one day.

"Oh, they told me it was OK to just take them when I got back to the ward on Monday," he said. I knew he was lying, and I was not having it.

"No, that's not how it works, and you know it. You've been skipping every weekend, haven't you? I told you before, and I am saying it again.

I am not going through this over and over again, and I can't believe you want to! If you want us to move back in together and start being a family again, you *must* take the medicines, Jeff, *and* keep appointments. I mean it!" I declared.

"Alright, Susie. Fine. Have it your way," he said.

"And while we're at it, I hate that you're smoking all the time now, Jeff. You know I had to grow up in a house full of cigarette smoke and I hate it. It makes me feel like I'm suffocating to breathe it. I will not have Nikki grow up with it!" I added, on a roll now. "Even though everyone on the ward seems to do it, you just need to find a way not to," I said, feeling more like a parent than a wife.

He didn't like that either but said nothing.

By the time he was nearing full transition from hospital to home, he was a changed man and not in a good way. He was no longer psychotic, but I hardly knew him. He was crude and insensitive; his conversations were defensive and derisive at the same time. He was not interested in current events and rarely expressed curiosity about his daughter's days, new words, or skills. His hair was long and oily, his fingers were staining yellow with tobacco, and it did not seem like his toothbrush had been much used. He reeked of cigarettes and hospital beds. On one of our final sessions with the social worker, I again implored him to commit to taking the medication consistently, on schedule, and attend every clinic visit. I made it clear it was the only way I would agree to us moving on as a couple. He vowed that he would and said he understood the consequences for our future. But mostly, I thought, he was saying what needed to be said to get his hospital discharge later that week.

I continued working as a nanny once Jeff transitioned to living at his parents' house full time, but I began spending occasional nights with him. He seemed to be taking his medications regularly, and I was trying to keep up my part of the bargain, remaking our little family, but with trepidation. Sometimes he was conversant and in tune with me and

Nikki, doing normal parental things with her like sitting patiently while she played in the bathtub or out in the tiny swimming pool or chasing her as she toddled along picking up bugs and leaves. Other times he was distant and unreachable by me or anyone.

CHAPTER 17

ROADS DIVERGE

Winter 1976 to Spring 1977,
San Antonio, Texas

Winter turned to spring that, in south Texas, means bluebonnets mixed with red Indian paintbrushes blooming along the side of the road. I picked pink buttercups from the yard and turned our noses yellow with pollen to Nikki's delight. I do not remember crying or dwelling on events of the recent past. Nor do I remember thinking about how wonderful my life would be in the future. I focused on my daughter, our family, and our safety. "Just keep putting one foot in front of the other," I remember saying to myself, and "Stay on your toes, and keep your eyes open!"

One Saturday morning I awoke to the insistent ringing of the doorbell at my parents' house. I had gotten away from Carolyn's late on Friday and decided to sleep there instead of going to the Greens' house. Mom came back to say that Jeff was at the front door, anxious to talk to me outside on the front lawn. I made sure Nikki was settled with her granny and went outside to find him agitated and pacing.

"You've got to come start living with *me* now, Susie! You're my wife, and you need to start acting like it! I'm out of the hospital now, so you can quit taking care of that other lady's kids and bring Nikki over to Mom and Dad's house," he demanded.

"OK, Jeff, we can talk about that for sure," I said slowly. "In fact, we already talked about the plan, right? We agreed that we would wait a few weeks to make sure you were doing good as an outpatient, and then we would figure out where to live together," I said, looking at him askance. "Have you missed some of your medications? Because you are acting upset like you do sometimes when—"

"It's none of your business what I do with my medicine!" Jeff interrupted. "In fact, that's the other thing I came to tell you! I've figured out it's the medicine that is making me crazy, and I'm not going to let you tell me what to do anymore! I don't even feel like a man when I take them. It's like bugs crawling under my skin constantly, and I can't stand it. You all are just using them to keep me down!

"Susie," he continued, "you wanna know the drugs that help me the most? Smoking pot and cigarettes! And I can get both of them real easy from my friend from the hospital! She don't care if I take the medicines or not, and she don't try to boss me around neither," he said, looking smug. "And she likes to visit me at Mom and Dad's house when you're not there."

I was speechless. He was choosing madness over a semblance of normal life with me and our baby. I was astounded that he had just admitted he was willing to throw away everything because he did not want to take some pills. My pride was stung as he threw out the news about a girlfriend from the hospital, which I suspected might have been the main purpose of his visit. He was rejecting me! The emotions of hurt and rejection washed over me and brought me to tears.

"Jeff," I said through tears running down my face, "I love you. You are my husband. You have been my best friend since high school. I took a marriage vow to stay with you in sickness and in health but not when you refuse help when you are sick. I will not throw away my life and the life of our child if you are not willing to do your part. I am not changing my mind about that. If that means you are leaving me so you don't have to take the medicine, then I guess you should go be with your hospital girlfriend."

"I guess I should then," he said. He got back in his car and burned rubber as he drove off.

I stood there staring at the retreating car as tears dried on my face, noting the dreary day and splatters of rain starting to pelt down. I walked back in the house to tell Mom and Dad what was going on and comfort Nikki who always knew when emotional things were afoot. But in the telling, I found my shock and tears turning to a bit of a smile as relief began to flood through me. I had laid out a reasonable path for the three of us, as the social worker had advised, a plan that was healthy and involved compromise by all but to which I was committed and to which Jeff had agreed. I was keeping my bargain and honoring our wedding vows. But here he was, voting with his feet and broadcasting his intentions. He was as sane as he had been for months, but he was clearly rejecting me and the road to sanity. Oh my, was I going to be set free?

Hallelujah, and amen!

Of course, my relationship with Jeff did not end once he declared he was not going to take his medicines and had a hospital girlfriend. When his mother learned what had happened, she started a campaign to get me back.

"Susie, you know he loves you. He didn't mean what he said. We'll make sure he takes his medicines," Malvis said.

"No, Malvis," I said, "he meant what he said; in fact, he's already shown it. He's stopped taking the medications even before he's fully discharged from the hospital!"

"Sweetheart, you know you love him. And you made a vow to God and the church to stay with him in sickness and in health. He's sick, and he needs your help." She cajoled, sweet-talked, and then laid on the guilt to get me to change my mind. Jeff became less boastful of his hospital "girlfriend" and started talking about how we should get back together. But I was done; having been through two years of hell and seen the specter of my future life if we stayed together, I let myself acknowledge feeling repulsed by the idea of being with him physically, emotionally, or legally. Under pressure from his family, he said he would take his medications and see the doctors, but I did not believe him and I did not want to be his mother, his nurse, or his jailer. I cried with Malvis because I loved her and would miss having her in my life. I was sad for Jeff, but I knew that our lives were forfeit if I went back. I started divorce proceedings.

I was ready to get my life in gear so Nikki and I could become independent while staying close to family for support. I told Carolyn the momentous events of the weekend and looked for her thoughts and advice. She knew my college degree was in the sciences, and she had a good friend whose husband was director of a research laboratory at the University of Texas, San Antonio, Health Sciences Center. She invited them over for drinks and dinner so I could meet them. Our dinner resulted in a formal interview with Dr. Blum and his senior laboratory technician, and by June, I was transitioning to a full-time lab position. Nikki and I moved our things out of Carolyn's house, and we started living with my parents.

During the day, Nikki stayed at a family-owned daycare while Mom, Dad, and I all worked, and then either Mom or I picked her up to come home where we shared meals, chores, and life together at their home. Mom and Dad were doting grandparents, and she loved having all three of us there to parent her. One evening they asked if they could watch Nikki at home the next day instead of me taking her to daycare.

"Fine by me!" I said, happy for a less stressful morning without getting both of us dressed and out the door early enough to drop her off, fight traffic, and get to work. When I arrived home that evening, Nikki was still napping, and they were sporting big grins and fancy clothes.

"Change your clothes," Dad said. "We're going out for dinner to celebrate!" I turned to Mom, surprised.

"We got married today! Again!" Mom said, beaming.

"And Nikki was our best girl and bridesmaid!" Dad said, equally smug. We hugged and I cried, and we went off to celebrate.

I enjoyed my new job, made new friends, and found old friends who had completed the medical technology program that I had abandoned two years earlier. I began volunteering at the San Antonio Free Clinic in the evening once a week, serving as an assistant to the third – and fourth-year medical students and their attending physician mentors. The clinic was in a gritty neighborhood in downtown San Antonio and provided medical services focused on diagnosing and treating sexually transmitted infections and family planning services, including abortion referrals, for indigent patients from local neighborhoods. I immensely enjoyed the patient interactions, felt privileged to be privy to their daily struggles, and fascinated by the complexities and messiness of everyone's lives. I also loved being able to make practical use of my biology and microbiology knowledge to help clients understand, in plain language, what was going on and how to prevent problems in the future.

By the fall of 1976, Jeff and I were officially divorced. My volunteer work at the clinic was more gratifying every week and convinced me that I wanted to pursue a medical career centered on patient care. Health educator? Nurse? I became friends with the medical students working at the free clinic, and we shared pitchers of beer at a local bar after the clinic closed. I also dated some of the men. As I got to know them, it dawned on me how similar we were: about the same age, organized, and hard working. They were smart, though not obviously any smarter than me. They did not have a toddler waiting at home for them, but otherwise they were peers who had spent the last two years focused on getting into medical school instead of hitchhiking across America, having a baby, and navigating the world of mental illness.

I pondered which career path to pursue, talking to friends and family about the possibilities. I recalled an event in my senior year of college when I accompanied friends to celebrate a classmate's acceptance to medical school. She was a biology major like me—I suppose she had been "premed," but I never paid much attention to that—and I knew that I ranked higher than her in class standing. At the celebration I remember thinking, *Wow, she must be a genius or something to have gotten into med school! I wonder how I never knew that.* I wondered how she was doing. And then, the penny dropped. Why couldn't I go to medical school and become a doctor?

I did the research to figure out what other class credits I needed to qualify for medical school entrance, what standardized tests I needed to study for and take, and what the timeline looked like. I figured that, even if I was competitive enough to get into med school as an older nontraditional student, it would be a minimum of three, maybe four, years before I could start medical school. That seemed like a very long time. Plus, I was a single mom living with my parents. They would be supportive, but would this be fair to them or to my daughter? I talked my ideas over with friends and family, but it was the senior lab supervisor, where I worked, who gave me the best perspective.

"Carol, that's a great idea! I mean I would have no interest in taking care of sick people—no way, I'm not nearly nice enough—but if that's what you want to do, you should do it!" he said.

"But I wouldn't even get started for probably four years," I said, "and then another four years of med school and three more for residency. It will be a decade or more before I get finished!"

"Guess what, Carol?" he said. "A decade is going to pass no matter what. That's how time works. What do you want to have accomplished at the end of that time? It's like what they say about the best time to plant a tree: a year ago! What's the next best time? Today! Will you look back after ten years and kick yourself for not following your dreams? Or will you have achieved something important at the end of the decade?" I was inspired by his advice and have often repeated it to others.

I began acting on my plan to apply to medical school. I enrolled in night classes to satisfy the University of Texas medical school system requirements and began to tell others about my goal. I bought books to study for the medical college admission test (MCAT) and researched the path toward becoming a doctor and career options beyond. But life had two more surprises in store for me. The first came about after being told that a certain clinical pharmacy doctoral candidate had his eye on me and hoped to ask me out at our department's upcoming Christmas party. I had seen him in the hallways and thought he was interesting looking in a prematurely balding, long-haired post-hippy kind of way. Our mutual friend's description of him as shy was an understatement, and at the party he avoided eye contact with me, nursing a bottle of beer while standing awkwardly next to his extroverted best friend who soaked up all the attention. I finally broke the ice and started talking to him, to get the ball rolling. After several monosyllabic responses, he mumbled out the anticipated invitation to go to dinner the next weekend. I said, "Sure! But right now, want to dance?" at which point he mumbled a quick goodbye and bolted from the room.

George took me to a lovely restaurant later the next week where I ate lobster for the first time and drank California wine that he ordered. Unbeknownst to either of us, my parents had decided to also splurge and were in another part of the restaurant with my daughter.

"Uh-oh!" I said, looking around with both delight and concern on my face. "That's my daughter we can hear in the other part of the dining room around the corner! If she sees me, she will not let me out of her sight without much wailing and gnashing of teeth!" I continued.

"Wait, you can tell from just what we heard a second ago that it is your daughter?" he asked, skepticism written on his face.

"Yep!" I said and then got up and peeked around the corner, catching my mom's eye and waving. Once they finished their meal, they exited the long way around, waving to me as they left. George was impressed that such a bond existed between a mother and child that I knew from just a peep that she was mine. He and I had great conversations and agreed to keep seeing each other. He had many loyal friends, all of whom made it clear to me that, if I broke his heart—this shy, quiet man who was a great friend to them—they would be very upset with me. He had been raised by his Mormon mother and his pharmacist business-owner father in central California, went to the University of Utah for undergraduate pharmacy school, and then to San Antonio for their clinical pharmacy doctoral program. His father had converted to Mormonism in the past few years (i.e., happy wife, happy life), and both parents were taciturn and strict but very supportive of their four kids. George and I professed no interest in religion and confessed that we were not sure if we even believed in God anymore.

We were both serious minded about a future as professionals and had similar middle-class values. He did not blink that I had a nearly-two-year-old child, and I thought it was probably fine that I liked him very much but was not in love with him. That pitter-patter of the heart thing was probably just a one-time event, I thought, and it had died with Jeff. I told him this, and he seemed to take it in stride. I had always heard that "still waters run deep," and I thought I could probably help him come out of his shell and over time grow deeper in love with this quiet man.

While our relationship was warming up, the next surprise was most unwelcome. My mother developed severe back pain that turned out to be vertebral bone metastases from the breast cancer. We were devastated, and I took time off to drive her to radiation therapy and spend as much time with her as I could. She let me know that her greatest concern was that I find someone to spend my life with, to make a home for our Nikki, and help me achieve my goals. She and Dad had met George, whom they saw as stable, smart, patient and kind with Nikki, and clearly in love with me. They thought I had finally met a worthy suitor!

We had only been dating a few weeks when, as winter turned to spring in 1977, George and I began talking about the idea of marriage. He was in his final semester of the doctoral program and had accepted a faculty position at the University of Utah School of Pharmacy. It would be an exciting opportunity and a new beginning for both of us. It was in Utah, land of Mormons, snow skiing, and outdoor excursions in both deserts and mountains of the West. I could go back to being a stay-at-home mom with Nikki while figuring out the medical school plan. I feared it was too soon, but we seemed to be a good complement for each other, and I was intensely anxious to get on with life at the side of someone competent and capable. Nikki seemed quite happy to play with him, and likewise he seemed comfortable with her.

One evening George came over, and Mom and I cooked dinner for the five of us. It was a warm and friendly time together, but as we were passing the dishes and beginning to dig into our food, there was an insistent pounding on the front door. Before we could get there, Jeff flung open the door, sporting a threatening gap-toothed smile. Nikki started grinning to see the familiar "Dada" person walk in. Dad got up from the table and started toward Jeff, while George also stood up, looking threatened and unsure but ready to help with whatever needed doing. Mom picked Nikki up out of the highchair and held her on her lap for safe-keeping, and Jeff plunked down in a chair at the table.

"Oh great! Y'all fixed dinner for me! And lookie there, we have some company! Who's this, Susie? Your new boyfriend? Who are you? I'm Jeff, the crazy husband, and that's my daughter! Hi, sweetie!" he said reaching for her. George responded with his name while keeping his eyes on Jeff.

"Jeff, we're just sitting down to dinner. You need to leave now and come back when it's a better time for us and you can spend time with

Nikki," I said, trying to be civil but firm and staying seated between him and where Mom had Nikki on her lap. Dad was not at all interested in being civil, but before he could say anything, Jeff picked up a sharp knife from the table and started jabbing it into the tabletop.

"I don't think so, Susie. I think little Georgie and I need to have a talk outside, see if he can take me on like he probably thinks he can," Jeff said, blustering and menacing.

And that was enough for my dad who walked behind Jeff and jerked the dining room chair out from under him, forcing Jeff to stumble and stand.

"Put down the goddamn knife, Jeff, and get the hell out of my house before I take you outside and knock the rest of the teeth out of your head!" he demanded, toe to toe with Jeff. Fred and Jeff were similar height, but Dad was heavier. More importantly, Fred had the authority of a father-in-law, and years of ingrained grudging respect took some of the wind out of Jeff's sails. George closed ranks with Dad, and the two of them corralled Jeff out of the front door, locking it once Jeff was pushed out, while I clutched the telephone threatening to call the police.

Figuring out how to navigate Jeff's mental instability, his rights as a father, and my new romantic relationship was getting complicated. Marrying George and moving to Utah sounded like a promising solution. George wanted to move ahead with the idea, but my mother had recently been hospitalized for a complication from the radiation. When she was feeling better, George paid her a visit and formally asked her and Dad for my hand in marriage. Her tears of joy took me by surprise.

"But Mom, it means we'll be far away," I said. Did she really think this was a good idea?

"That's why there are cars and airplanes!" she said. "You need to go live your life and follow your dream to become a doctor! And this man loves you and will keep you both safe. But only if you promise that you get my grandbaby on the phone with me every single week so she never forgets her granny's voice."

"Of course, Mom," I said, brushing away my own tears. I took her hand in mine and brought it to my lips.

"Don't cry, now," she said. "Just spread your wings and go, sweetheart! Follow your dreams, and don't ever hold back again! Not for anyone!"

I thought then that my mother was putting my happiness before hers, and I was enormously grateful. I know now that my happiness was her happiness. That's how moms are.

Thank you, Mama. I'm still flying!

AFTERWORD

*1977–1992, Salt Lake City, Utah,
and Durham, North Carolina*

Nikki celebrated her second birthday in May of 1977 and, a week later, George and I married with a few friends and family at the Japanese Sunken Gardens in San Antonio, followed by a large party at George's place with friends, family, kegs of beer, and live music. Later that summer, we moved to Utah and started our new lives. I loved the geography of Salt Lake City, with the Wasatch mountains, cold bubbling streams, and clear mountain lakes. I loved the novelty of snow and learned to downhill ski. My daughter also loved the snow and became an intrepid little skier. She wanted to be outdoors as much as possible, even when it seemed bitterly cold to me. I made new friends and eventually got a job at the Utah State Department of Health. My life was getting back on track, and I was ready to *go*! But rather than ecstatic joy, I experienced wrenching sadness and tears, reliving the events that had transpired with Jeff and worrying about my mother, whom I had just left, again, in San Antonio.

I recalled the times when people saw me navigating pregnancy, college, and Jeff's mental illness and marveled, saying, "Susie, I just don't know how you do it! You always look like you've got it under control. How do you stay so positive?" I didn't really have a good answer, so I would shrug and say something like, "What choice do I have?" But the truth was I was doing what people do in crisis mode—focusing all my energy on the immediate needs of safety, shelter, food, and water for self and family. I had no room for anything else while I was in crisis mode. But once I was safe in Utah, I cried, and I cried.

I became a stay-at-home mom again, which is what I had always intended to do, just like my mama had done with me. But in the preceding year, I had become a very efficient working mom, used to conversing with adults all day and then enjoying precious hours with my toddler in the evening. Nikki had become accustomed to having playmates at her daycare all day, and that's what she expected me to be now. While endless hours of playing Candyland was fun for her at first, surprisingly, neither of us were as happy in the supposed idyllic situation as we thought we would be. Specifically, I was not busy enough to keep the memories and emotions at bay.

"Carol, Carol, wake up! Why are you crying? Are you hurting?" George asked.

"I have to check on Nikki. I'll be right back," I said, getting out of bed, wiping tears from my face, relieved to see her little butt sticking up in the air as she slept soundly in the next room.

"I had such a horrible dream, George," I said. "Nikki was playing outside, making a snowman, and I thought you were with her, but then you were in the kitchen, and I went outside and immediately I knew she was gone, and I knew it was Jeff and he had taken her, and we couldn't find her . . ."

The nightmare nights were interspersed with sleepless nights when I ruminated about how Jeff indeed might make his way to our house and kidnap her or how Nikki might have inherited his condition and develop schizophrenia herself, a concern that plagued me until she was safely into her twenties with no sign of psychosis.

Poor George suffered the brunt of my grief and anguish. When he came home from work, I would badger him to talk about the details of his day and the people he interacted with, trying to get myself out of my funk. But talking about himself was not his strong suit and never would be. I would eventually lash out in frustration and then feel guilty and finally let the dam burst and start talking about what memory had been occupying my mind all day, sobbing as I relived scenes from the recent past. Though he was good at listening, he didn't know what to do or say, and like me, he did not realize how normal my reaction was.

"Carol, it's alright, honey. You're safe now; you are with me, and we are far away from San Antonio. What can I do that would help?" he would ask, rubbing his bald head while I sobbed, trying to hold my hand and comfort me, with no success. I would eventually go to the bedroom and bury my head in a pillow until the storm passed and my tears dried up.

I remember apologizing to George often in those days.

"It's not you," I said, "and I do not understand why I'm crying *now*! I went through hell for two years and hardly ever cried. Not every day, that's for sure. And after Jeff and I divorced, I went to work at the lab every day, came home, and enjoyed my daughter, my friends and family, went on dates, dealt with Jeff when he showed up, and I didn't fall apart then either. Why the hell am I falling apart now when everything's fine?"

In addition to being sad, I was also angry but couldn't figure out who or what I was angry at. I felt angry at God and got bolder about saying I no longer believed in Him. But that didn't help much, because how could I be mad at someone or something I didn't believe in? I was angry at Jeff, but he was the victim as much as I, so that didn't seem fair. He did not choose to become psychotic, right? Nevertheless, his actions had been real and scary and hurtful, and I was having a hard time not hating him for what he put us through. And he remained a threatening force I had to worry about every day. But I also felt guilty for divorcing him and leaving him with his demons. It was an emotional conundrum.

In retrospect, what I was going through was a completely normal reaction to recent trauma. Today we would say that I was experiencing post-traumatic stress and acknowledge that it was normal for my psyche to wait until all was safe to process the events I had been through, feel the emotions I had kept in check, and grieve over what had happened to me and what I had lost. Unfortunately, I did not seek professional counseling until years later, so I did not talk through the events and grieve over them in any systematic way. Instead, I leaned on work and family distractions and new close friends who helped me heal. I also focused on getting things done to pursue my goal of medical school. In other words, I compartmentalized my pain and grief.

I also worried constantly about my mom and had dreams about her dying and about being at her funeral. I tormented myself by remembering times I had been unthoughtful or unkind to her as a teenage girl or recently when I had not realized the extent of her pain with the recurrent cancer. I spoke with her often, but it did not replace the intimacy of daily conversations and, more recently, living with her and sharing the love and delight in watching her with her granddaughter.

I spoke to my mother at least once a week and held the phone for Nikki who squealed in happiness to talk to her granny. I got her to send recipes for my favorite meals, like her enchiladas and pinto beans, and sought her advice for weaning Nikki from the bottle, chiding myself that I had not weaned her from the breast directly to a cup. I probably told her about my crying jags, but I do not remember for sure. If I did, she probably said something like "It will take some time, Susie, but you'll get over it."

Photo 14: Nikki with her Granny before we moved to Utah.

I saw my mother one last time, in October of 1977, when she and Dad came to visit at the height of the most beautiful season of the year in Utah, with aspen trees and hardwoods standing ablaze across the mountains. The bastard cancer had spread to the back of her eye, explaining sudden light sensitivity and pain. She could barely keep her eyes open when outside in the daylight and was puffy from the steroids she was taking to reduce internal swelling. Her skin was ashen colored, and she had constant pain from the metastases but was immensely happy to be holding her granddaughter in her arms again.

"I hope they let you into medical school soon, Susie," Mom said when visiting, "because you need to figure out a cure for cancer so it doesn't steal other people's lives! I want to see this little one grow up!"

We made plans for me to visit in the spring, but she had sudden abdominal pain and internal bleeding from a prednisone-induced stomach ulcer and had to be admitted to a San Antonio hospital in early

February. Dad called as soon as she was out of surgery and said she was resting comfortably but that I should make plans to visit soon. I made plane reservations for later that week. But the dreaded call came later that night.

"Susie, it's Dad. She's gone, honey. She's gone now," he said, breaking down.

"What happened, Dad? I thought she was going to be fine for a while, after the surgery! I made plane reservations and I'll be there this weekend!" I argued, desperately wanting him to take it back, say I wasn't too late to say goodbye.

"I was there after surgery until she was sleeping. They had to give her lots of blood, but the nurses told me I should go home and rest and let her sleep. So, I did, but then the doctor called and said the stitches they used to stop the bleeding must have come loose, like they can do when someone has been on a lot of prednisone, because she was bleeding internally again. They asked me what they should do. The doctor said she was semi-conscious at that point, but he wasn't sure the surgeon could repair the damage if he went back in and didn't think it would give her much more time anyway, because the cancer has spread so far. I said I needed to come be with her and not to do anything till I got there. I think she knew I was there; she squeezed my hand a little and I sat next to her. She was peaceful but so pale, and I didn't think she should suffer anymore and then she was gone, Susie. Just like that, she was gone," he finished, crying softly into the phone.

I cried, I sobbed, I shook my head in denial that she could be gone, that my rock, my soul, the creator of my being, my mother was not on this earth anymore could not be true. It could not be. But it was.

When Nikki and I moved from San Antonio to Utah in the summer of 1977, I made a conscious effort to always be honest with her about Jeff, explaining what was going on with him as best I could, according to her age and maturity level. I wanted her to think of him with compassion, but

I also needed her to understand that he could not be trusted if he were to suddenly show up at her daycare or at our home. I did not want her frightened of him, but having experienced a near-miss of violence during my pregnancy and his attempted kidnapping at Carolyn's house a year earlier, I could not be complacent either. We made sure the schools always knew that he was persona non grata and cautioned Nikki never to go anywhere with a stranger or with her dad, Jeff, unless we were there with her.

In the first few years after we left San Antonio, he made threats about coming to Utah to see her and "take her on a trip." Early in his course of chronic schizophrenia, he was still intellectually and physically capable of doing so. So, in the spirit of keeping your friends close and your enemies closer, I spent time talking with him whenever he called, asking where he was calling from and trying to determine his mental state. I also called and spoke with his mother regularly, and we had an understanding that, if she thought he was headed our direction, she would contact me. When he called our house I would talk with him, giving him some details of Nikki's life, and if he was not too agitated or fragmented, I would get her on the phone to talk to him.

Conversation was strange, and his tangents were hard for an adult to follow, much less a five – or ten-year-old child. Sometimes when he called and I answered the phone, without preamble he would launch into a description about what the voices had recently been telling him to do. For example, one time he told me the voices told him to swallow a wad of crushed up glass. He started to obey but his family intervened, and he headed back to the hospital for another commitment stay. Eventually we tried to convince Jeff to allow George to legally adopt Nikki, but he refused. I fretted about what might happen if I died; would the legal system send Nikki to be raised by Jeff or Jeff's family? The thought filled us with dread. We hired an attorney to pursue adoption.

"Carol, George, I recommend you not spend any time or money working on adoption," the lawyer stated with certainty.

"Legally, Jeff has not purposely abandoned Nikki. He is ill and unable to support or care for her. You are telling me that he calls and tries to stay in touch and would probably state that he would like to do more, except you moved out of state. A judge would never involuntarily terminate his parental rights precisely because of his mental illness. It's a catch-22—even if Jeff agreed to terminate his rights, the judge would doubt that Jeff was mentally competent to make such a decision!" he stated.

"No, your best course is to change your daughter's last name to match yours and George's and to clearly state in your will that you want her to remain in George's custody if something were to happen to you, Carol," he said, "and stay healthy until she is of majority age!"

We visited my family in San Antonio about once a year and made sure to see Jeff and his family on most of those visits. Malvis, my beloved mother-in-law, was found to have metastatic colon cancer eight years after we moved to Utah, and she died in 1985. Jeff then lived with his father, both sharing a trailer on his brother's property "in the country" outside San Antonio. When my daughter was a teenager, I gave her the option of whether to keep seeing Jeff on our regular visits to San Antonio. By the time she was fourteen or fifteen years old, Jeff had been in and out of mental hospitals many times and had an immobile right arm, a result of local police shooting him when he refused to give up the Bowie knife that he was carrying down the sidewalk in a south side San Antonio neighborhood. His fingers and teeth were stained brownish yellow from two to three packs per day of cigarette smoking, and he reeked of tobacco and infrequent baths. He could not sit still, rocking front to back, front to back, a continuing side effect from the anti-psychotic drugs now firmly rooted in his nervous system. She had a hard time carrying on a conversation with him as he fidgeted, smoked, and suddenly started laughing about some bizarre thought that had captured his attention. Nikki decided it was too painful and awkward to try to keep up the pretense of a relationship, and I supported her decision.

A few months after moving to Utah, I got a job as a disease control specialist at the Utah Department of Health. This was my introduction to public health, and I had the good fortune to work with Centers for Disease Control (CDC)-trained program managers and field epidemiologists. I was in the Utah State Immunization Program and travelled to counties throughout the state helping them monitor and improve their programs. We investigated and intervened in outbreaks such as measles and pertussis (whooping cough). I visited homes of families who were obviously polygamists and fringe religious groups living on the borders of the state, bringing immunizations to their children, no questions asked. I worked with my friends in the sexually transmitted disease (STD) section where we learned how to effectively question a person to get a more comprehensive list of their sexual contacts (e.g., "What, a good-looking guy like you, only five different partners in the past week? Come on, man! You must be forgetting a few quickies in the park!") and did pop-up epidemiology work at the burgeoning gay bar scene in downtown Salt Lake City. I also helped investigate the frightening outbreak of a new condition called toxic shock syndrome where healthy young women were dying of what looked like overwhelming sepsis from no obvious source. We helped collect the data that determined that the newly marketed high-absorbency tampons were allowing toxin-producing staphylococci to flourish and make the women sick, sometimes leading to death. In the meantime, Gary, my main supervisor in the immunization division, regaled me with stories of his time in Bangladesh working on the smallpox eradication campaign. My interest in going to medical school grew steadily.

I developed friendships in Utah that have lasted a lifetime. Meeting for drinks in the evening and sharing girlfriend stories allowed me to start healing. We were outspoken and smart and ready to take on the world. Soon my friend Susan and I started an annual "all women's camping and drinking adventure" group, with Nikki attending as the youngest inaugural member, and next included our friend, Connie. Slowly the annual gathering grew as new friendships developed. The requirements to attend were not very healthy or politically correct by today's standards, but it fit our brash attitude at the time. Each of us would bring munchies and drinks (or smokes or brownies) of choice to a local lake, usually arriving on a Friday night, and we would windsurf, sail, swim, beach walk, drink, talk, laugh, and repeat until Sunday afternoon.

As the memories of my trauma became less raw, I smiled more and cried less. George, Nikki, and I enjoyed the natural beauty of Utah, camping and hiking as often as possible, skiing in winters and working on our backyard garden in summer. George's colleagues from the college of pharmacy and their spouses formed another important group of friends.

I applied to medical school but was rejected the first time around and considered abandoning the idea and going to nursing school to become a nurse midwife since I had had such a good experience with Ms. Hoffmaster. But that was not really my dream, and George knew me well enough to counsel against it.

Photo 15: Nikki and I at one of many beautiful places in Utah where we camped and hiked as often as possible.

"Carol," George said when I floated the idea of nursing school, "I'm trying to imagine you taking orders from some guy who gets to make all the decisions because he has an MD behind his name, especially once you have a few years' experience. God help him!"

"You will be frustrated beyond belief!" he amended.

"Right, and probably a grade-A bitch at home," I said. "OK, let me retake the MCAT test."

So, I reapplied the next year and, while awaiting a decision, took a new job with Dr. Mark Skolnick, a University of Utah geneticist who, along with Dr. Mary-Claire King at the University of California, Berkely, was trying to find a gene that explained high rates of breast cancer in some families. Utah, with its large population of Mormon families who, for religious purposes, collect and store genealogical information, was an enormous asset to such research. I served as one of Dr. Skolnick's study coordinators and contacted family members to enroll in our study. The work led to the eventual discovery of the BRCA-1 and BRCA-2 genes. Eventually Skolnick went on to found Myriad Genetics, and he and King attained numerous scientific and professional awards and accolades.

In the summer of 1981, I was accepted for admission to the University of Utah School of Medicine, to begin that fall. It was hard work, but I loved it and thrived. George was supportive, but my six-year-old daughter had reservations. She started first grade while I started medical school, and she was not thrilled with having to share her mother's attention, first with the new husband/dad and then with medical school. It was hard for both of us. She felt deprived of my full attention when I was studying or on call, and I felt deprived because I had to rush home to spend every minute I could with her before diving into the books or driving back to the hospital.

Saying medical school was hard is like saying going through childbirth, or child rearing for that matter, is hard. The words barely scrape the surface of the intensity of the experience. I thought I was a good student before, but I realized I must have glided through college on a breeze com-pared to the amount of studying that I had to do in medical school. It did not help that I had been out of college for five years before starting medical school, either. I was out of practice. Plus, entire fields of biology had been born or turned upside down in the interim! Though it was hard, I was proud to see what I was accomplishing. My friends and family were happy for me, though it was hard for some to wrap their heads around, including my own father!

"Susie, I'm so proud of you! But what exactly does it mean that you are now in 'medical school'?" I remember him asking more than once. "I was trying to explain to my golf buddies the other day, and well, does that mean you'll be a nurse when you're finished, or what, exactly?"

"No, Dad, it means I will be an MD, medical doctor, physician, just like our old family doctor, Dr. Richmond, or your current doctor, Dr. McCracken," I replied, somewhere between exasperation and amuse-ment. I had already gotten similar comments from some of my patients whose thought process seemed to be "She's a woman working in the hos-pital, so she must be a nurse." But just before my graduation, it seemed to have sunk in, and after he watched me take the Hippocratic oath and walk across the stage to receive my diploma he beamed and couldn't stop telling everybody to make no mistake—his daughter was *a doctor*!

"Your mama would be so proud," he said. And that was true.

*Photo 16: Daughter Nikki started first grade at the same time
I started medical school.*

As medical school was concluding, George and I interviewed around the country to figure out where we wanted to go next so I could continue my medical training and he could advance his clinical pharmacy career. We settled on a move to Durham, North Carolina, where he took a new faculty position at the University of North Carolina, and I began an internal medicine internship and residency training at Duke University. The Duke Internal Medicine training program had a well-deserved reputation of being rigorous, with a grueling on-call schedule and excellent faculty. Even more importantly, my co-interns and residents were wicked smart, dedicated to their patients and to helping each other succeed. We always had each other's backs.

I was very proud to be a "Duke marine" under the leadership of Drs. Joe Greenfield and Ralph Corey. And I jumped at the chance to stay at Duke for subspecialty fellowship training in infectious diseases. I was primed for this specialty from my days of public health in Utah, and now there was a new disease in the world that had a nearly 100 percent fatality rate for those infected. It was a sneaky virus that lived silently within its human host for years, spreading to new sexual partners, to babies while still in their infected mother's womb, and to anyone who was exposed to their blood. Eventually the disease showed its hand in the form of previously rare or unknown secondary or opportunistic infections that dragged the infected host through two to four final years of misery and then death.

The acquired immunodeficiency syndrome (AIDS) was first recognized in 1981, the year I started medical school in Utah. The first population to be affected were otherwise healthy young gay men, and then injection drug users, and then people who had received lots of blood products, like those with hemophilia. When I first thought of specializing in infectious diseases, I wanted to study and treat diseases common outside the US, diseases like malaria and African sleeping sickness, often referred to as neglected tropical diseases. But the more I learned and experienced in Zimbabwe and then Tanzania, the more obvious it became that the human immunodeficiency virus (HIV), which causes AIDS, was exploding in sub-Saharan Africa and causing a secondary epidemic of tuberculosis, which was killing young and old, whether they had HIV or not. I received training in general infectious diseases at Duke while also studying and then doing research with our Duke program in Dar es Salaam and later Moshi, Tanzania. I served as a Duke-trained physician scientist and infectious diseases expert for most of my career before transitioning to full-time global public health work for the final ten years of my career with a global nonprofit, FHI360, based in Durham, North Carolina.

It took ten years for me to reach my goal of becoming a fully trained physician, but just as my former lab supervisor said, the time was going to pass anyway, and I was glad that I had used it to reach my goal. I had also raised my daughter in a stable, loving home, and George and I had established homes and sets of friends in Utah and then in North Carolina. I was five years older than my peers in medical school and residency so that, by the time I finished, I already had a child in high school while they were just getting married and starting families. My career was about to take off.

Unfortunately, once the all-consuming rigor of medical school, residency, and fellowship concluded, some of my unhappiness and restlessness from earlier in my marriage to George returned. I was often angry and short-tempered with him, though I couldn't figure out why.

"I am married to the world's nicest man," I said to the psychotherapist when I first engaged with her. "Just ask anyone and they will confirm this. But I am miserable, and I do not understand it. Please fix me!"

I shouldn't have been surprised that most of the sessions over the next two years focused on processing earlier life events. We started by dissecting my reaction over my father's leaving the family when I was seventeen years old, and I learned that my subsequent teenaged marriage to Jeff was a classic way to try to reestablish my broken nest. If it had happened two or three years later, I probably would not have reacted so precipitously. We then went into the trauma of life with Jeff during his dive into insanity, and I learned that my grief and anger once I was out of danger were also part of a natural response to a traumatic situation. It was reassuring to have my reactions of pain, fear, resentment, and anger articulated, acknowledged, and validated. But what did this have to do with George?

"Carol, have you considered perhaps that George is just not 'the one' for you?" my therapist asked sometime in our second year of working together.

"Not that I think there is only one person for each of us," she said, "but there does need to be enough passion, magnetism, spark, glue—whatever you want to call it—to make people stay happy in a marriage over the long haul. I haven't heard you talk about ever having that with him. Tell me about when you were first together. Was it all-consuming, on-fire, or . . . How was it?"

"No, not at all," I said. "I worried about this and talked to George about it when we were dating and started talking about marriage. I told him I thought I loved him, but it was a calm, mature love, not the pitter-patter of the heart kind of love. I told him maybe that was just a once-in-a-lifetime thing and maybe only for teenagers. I thought I would never feel that way again after Jeff. He seemed to take it in stride."

We continued to explore this theme, and eventually I concluded that my rationale for marrying George was well intentioned – believing, as I did, that our interest in helping each other get on with our lives would be enough to sustain us – but was not enough to sustain a marriage over the long haul. Singer/songwriter Hayes Carll says it well: "We got the life that we wanted, not the love that we need."

George was hurt and confused by our divorce, since he had not done anything wrong. Fortunately, he quickly found someone else to share his life, and they have been married close to thirty years now. Happily, I found that the heart can go pitter-patter again, and when I found the one who made it happen, I held on tight.

REFLECTIONS ON MADNESS AND BELIEF

Winter 2023

I was fortunate to have the opportunity to learn about and process Jeff's mental illness as a physician and as a psychotherapy patient. As a medical student, I learned about schizophrenia and other "major" or "severe" psychiatric conditions. The list is topped by those that feature psychosis, defined as a collection of symptoms that indicate that the person is experiencing a complete break with reality. Intrusive thoughts and visual or auditory hallucinations are the hallmark of psychoses and are extremely real to the sufferer. The thoughts and voices bully the sufferer, exhorting him or her to perpetrate harm against themselves or others on threat of even worse harm if exhortations are not obeyed. Sufferers become convinced that people or animals or aliens are coming for them, preparing to harm them, i.e., they become paranoid. Paranoia leads to various levels of fright and agitation, which are normal reactions to real threats, but seem crazy to those of us not hearing or seeing what they are seeing.

The person experiencing a psychotic mental illness generally does not enter the psychotic phase all at once and stay there. Early on they recognize that the intrusive thoughts or hallucinations are probably not real and keep them hidden. They live many hours each day in a state of reality, acting rationally to real threats or acts of kindness, for example. But the oscillations between reacting normally and reacting to their own internal horror show make it very confusing for law enforcement as well as friends and families who think to themselves, *If he can act sane in the setting of X, he must be choosing to act insanely in situation Y.* I saw time and again that, once I understood the fundamentally crazy, delusional idea in Jeff's head, his downstream actions and emotions were appropriate and even clever. Imagine how horrible the voices must have been for him to take what he thought was the obvious best course of action: pull out his own tooth to eliminate the conduit to his brain.

Schizophrenia and bipolar disorder (formerly called manic-depressive illness) are two of the most common mental illnesses characterized by psychotic symptoms. Psychotic mental illnesses occur in societies and cultures across the globe and have similar recognizable features. Years after my life with Jeff, during my internal medicine training, I worked for nearly three months in Zimbabwe at a rural hospital south of Mutare, and during one of our field trips, I was able to diagnose a Zimbabwean woman with schizophrenia after less than ten minutes of conversation with her. I was working in a remote village when she approached me boldly, with the classic psychotic stare: eyes opened a little too wide, face and posture a little too aggressively forward. She was talking rapidly in English, in paragraphs that at first sounded brilliant but on closer listening turned out to be nonsense. Thinking I had made a brilliant diagnostic discovery, I confided my tentative diagnosis to the village elders.

"Thank you very much, Dr. Carol," the interpreter told me as the headman stood before me talking.

"Yes, she is the daughter of my eldest son, and the doctors in Mutare have told us that she has a certain disease, like what you say," he continued. "But she refuses to take the medicines they sent her home with. Our N'anga (traditional healer) gives her teas and special herbs, which help, but he has not been able to cast off her spell yet. We have built this special place for her," he stated, indicating a one-room mud and thatch hut that could be locked from the outside. I was a bit appalled at the idea of her being held captive in such a space, but he continued.

"Sometimes she walks off into the bush, which is very dangerous here. At night, it is easy to step on a large thorn [from the acacia trees] or, worse, a cobra or black mamba. During the day she has gone missing for days, and we have found her nearly dead with thirst," he continued, explaining that now, if she were to get too agitated, they would lock her inside to keep her safe.

Schizophrenia can look different depending on a particular person's underlying personality, cultural backdrop, and religious beliefs. One person's illness might be characterized by paranoia about the government, or perceived family or work-place enemies, or even space aliens who they think are tapping into their thoughts. In Jeff's case, his religious beliefs became fodder for the disordered thinking of the illness, and his increasing obsession with "following the Lord" at all costs was a symptom of the disease's progression, though of course being religious, per se, is not synonymous with mental illness.

Jeff's mother, Malvis, always harkened back to his bout of hepatitis as a potential cause for his illness, though there is no evidence of such a connection. I remember, though, the visual hallucination he described at that time of seeing an angel in his bedroom and wonder if this was the harbinger of cracks in his normal thought processes. I think his first full schizophrenic break occurred when we were at the airport near Seattle when he went missing all those hours. I imagine my plan to leave him and go back home set up an impossible conflict for him, pitting the sane, loving, common-sense husband, who still existed in good measure, against the increasingly demanding delusional voice in his head. The result left him nearly catatonic on the streets of Seattle and for weeks to follow. By coming back together as a husband-wife unit and getting back to our families, he was able to pull himself back to a semblance of sanity for several months while we were on the second hitchhiking trip.

I also think that the nature of our spiritual quest and our existential unmooring from the religion he had grown up with allowed him to go farther down the road of madness undetected than if we had been living a more traditional life. As it was, we were regularly talking to people who believed they spoke to a Christian god or Buddha during prayer or chanting or to the Great Spirit with the help of peyote. We read about and talked with those who believed swamis and other ascetics could really do "astral projection," or time travel. We intersected frequently with Pentecostal or "charismatic" Christians who believed that the Holy Ghost filled them and gave them the ability speak in other tongues. In this context, I can imagine Jeff justifying the voices he was hearing as yet another version of how God might speak to a faithful servant. His increasingly elaborate God/Satan belief system did not seem so strange, at least for a while.

People in the throes of acute schizophrenia need diagnosis, safety, care, and treatment. Most never act violently to others, but occasionally they are truly dangerous. I had no idea how much danger I was in during those days with Jeff, but knowing what I do now, I shudder at what my fate could have been. My heart aches for the people who are harmed by someone in the throes of acute schizophrenic and also for the families of those who perpetrate violence. They must navigate a host of complicated emotions: anguish and grief for their ill child and their future in prison or, less awful, a mental institution; horror at the violence they committed; disbelief that somehow no one saw what was coming or kept them from acting out their delusions.

I kept speaking with Jeff over the years until we were in our mid-forties and I remarried and moved away from Durham. At that point, I decided not to reach out with my new contact information so did not speak with him in the twenty or so years before his death in 2013 at age sixty-three. I spoke with his brother Kim and learned that Jeff lived with his family the rest of his life and had their physical and emotional support until he died. I imagine that Jeff suffered much of his life, tortured by intrusive, hateful, and negative thoughts, some of which caused him physical harm, and by the aggravating side effects of anti-psychotic medications. He did nothing to deserve the illness that plagued him, and thinking about it still makes me very sad.

I have been married for over twenty-five years to John Hamilton, my third husband, and we are living an idyllic life among the pines and hardwoods of central North Carolina. We retired from fulfilling and successful careers as physicians and infectious diseases experts and have the wherewithal to live life comfortably and on our own terms. We get to spend time with John's two children and grandchildren and enjoy hearing about their interesting lives. My daughter Nikki is an insightful, caring, and beautiful daughter and mother and a talented artist. Her child, my grandchild "Z," is the light of my life, like Nikki was to my mother and father. John and I were able to support them while Z went through difficult cancer treatment a few years ago. Both are back to living independent lives, at work and in college, but it was a question from Z during one of our lively family dinners that made me get serious about writing about this period of my life.

"So, Grandma, did you take a gap year in college?" Z asked, a seemingly simple question.

"Well, kind of," I said. "I went on a spiritual quest after my third year of college. I was already married to your biological grandfather, Jeff, who you've heard us talk about, and we hitchhiked around the country off and on for most of one year. We had lots of adventures and some scary times. I returned to college after the year of hitchhiking, but even then, my senior year in college was . . . dramatic. Jeff had what most people would call a mental breakdown; he became psychotic." I paused and took a swallow or two of wine.

"Did you know he locked me in a room when I was a few months pregnant with your mom, pulled out a Bowie knife, and announced he had to cut the baby out of my belly?" I asked. Z's eyes widened, and I went on to tell more stories from that time.

"So," I continued, "I guess the answer is, yes. Unconventional as it was, I took a gap year in college."

"And that was before you went to medical school?" Z asked.

"Yep!" I said.

"Geez, Grandma, how'd you do it? You ought to write some of that stuff down!"

I thought about me at age twenty-three and the road I found myself on with Jeff. Somehow, I managed to get off that trajectory and set us on one I thought would lead to something better, something more. How did I do it?

First, I had good luck. I was born to a stable home with loving parents who did not need to battle prejudice, deep poverty, addictions, or mental illness. I was born with an organized mind and a happy disposition, with enough intelligence to do well in school. I had enough innate fear of the unknown to shun drugs and alcohol as a youth. I had good friends, especially strong women friends, and caring teachers whom I turned to for help. They believed in me and gave me a hand when I needed it.

I also had an abiding belief . . . in myself. I embraced a stubbornness to succeed, which I credit my parents for instilling in me from infancy and my mother for reminding me of in her final months of life. Growing up, when things did not go exactly how I expected, I could usually figure out another way to achieve my goal, by studying longer, practicing more, walking farther, or working harder. I was also highly motivated by words of praise from my teachers and parents. I cared what they thought and wanted to please them. Success begat success, and by the time I was in high school, I was not afraid to dream big and not too put off by temporary setbacks.

On the contrary, my willingness to turn control over to a higher power and belief that with enough prayer, God would somehow come to our rescue was not helpful to me. In fact, I think it nearly cost me my life. How very different our lives would have been if I had not taken to heart the social worker's admonition to set boundaries. She empowered me to believe in my intuition and moral compass, to believe that my life and my dreams were as important as Jeff's.

And finally, I persisted. I refused to give up.

I held close my parents' mantra: "You can do anything you set your mind to, Susie!"

I saw *The Little Engine That Could*, bellowing blue-grey smoke at each difficult juncture, puffing up the hill, and around the bend saying, "I think I can; I think I can."

And I did.

ACKNOWLEDGEMENTS

Thank you to my husband, John, who has consistently encouraged me in every aspect of my professional and personal life and to my daughter, Nikki, who offered specific, thoughtful critique and a cherished comment: "Thank you for saving us, Mom."

I appreciate my grandchild, Z, who inspired me to write about this period of my life and then offered the following encouragement after reading an early draft: "Once I got past the boring stuff, like you were born and all that, I couldn't put it down!" Hopefully I have gotten rid of most of the boring stuff. Michael Denneny provided important developmental edits and helped build confidence in my voice (rest in peace, Michael), while Toni Lopopolo gave a few pivotal pointers and directed me toward authors who could improve my craft of writing. My cousins Martha and Barbara were my touchstones for what it was like when we were growing up in San Antonio, Texas, in the 1950s and 1960s, and Cousin Niels provided a welcome bridge between professional editing and familial advice.

Finally, our early church and then hitchhiking companion, Charlie, has been generous with his time and insights to help me remember key events and understand elements of our relationship I was oblivious to at the time. He and I remain distrustful of organized religion and religious leaders. But while I no longer believe in a god per se, Charlie lives an ever more focused life filled with prayer and love toward his Father God and son, Jesus Christ. We agree to disagree and treasure the memories of an intense time in our lives. Thank you, Charlie.

ABOUT THE AUTHOR

Dr. Carol Hamilton's grandmother traversed the plains of south Texas in a covered wagon in the late 1880s and settled in San Antonio, where Carol grew up in the 1950s and '60's. She graduated from Incarnate Word College despite a harrowing first marriage, chronicled in her memoir, *Hitchhiking to Madness*. She remarried and moved with her young daughter to Utah and worked in public health and genetics research before starting medical school in 1981.

She completed her medical training at Duke University Medical Center in Internal Medicine and Infectious Diseases. Carol spent 35 years as a practicing physician doing patient care (mostly HIV/AIDS and tuberculosis), research and teaching at Duke, and has over one hundred peer-reviewed scientific publications and awards for research, public health, and teaching. She spent the last 10 years of her career at FHI360 collaborating with colleagues in Africa and Asia to improve care for people with TB and AIDS. Carol has won numerous prestigious awards including the University of Utah's 2024 Distinguished Alumni Award from the Spencer Fox Eccles School of Medicine.

She is now an Emeritus Professor at Duke and continues to teach, helping younger doctors find their calling in the field of Infectious Diseases.

Carol considers herself a lifelong learner and currently studies oil painting and writing. She is also an avid birder and conservationist and leads the local Audubon chapter. She takes full advantage of Osher Lifelong Learning Institute (OLLI) at Duke as a teacher and a student learning about such topics as astrophysics, soul music, and human anthropology. Carol and her husband have four children and three grandchildren between them and enjoy living near Durham, North Carolina. To learn more or contact Carol, visit www.carolhamiltonmd.com.